The Bark of the Cony

Not If, But How
A Philosophy of Life

George Nash Smith

1-30-21

Peter,

Thank you for all you
do to help people get
outdoors.

I hope you enjoy
our stories

All the best,

Cody

All of the Climbing Smiths' net proceeds from this edition of The Bark of the Cony will be donated to The Climbing Smiths Foundation, which supports the preservation of nature, and organizations which foster leadership and self-reliance in the outdoors.

Copy Editor: Deirdre Stoelzle.
Cover and Interior Design: Stewart A. Williams.

Print ISBN: 978-1-7358203-0-9

Library of Congress Control Number: 2020918477

To my mother, Katherine Zurick (Mrs. F. Tupper) Smith, who taught me not to feel sorry for myself, and how to persist. She passed away in the year 2000 at the age of 104.

TABLE OF CONTENTS

CHAPTERS

Acknowledgments

Thanks to Judy Taylor, Butch Pritchett, Cynthia Nay, Dennis and Peggy Pluim, Richard Dudley and Barry Chamberlain for their input on this book.

Meaningful relationships are important towards having a fulfilled life. I have life-long friendships with fellow Eagle Scouts from Troop 1 in Denver. We believe we coined the motto, "Winners never quit and quitters never win," in 1946 when we formed "ETO," Eagles of Troop One. Thanks go to my friends, Bob Swerer, who taught me how to play the guitar, Warren Pulis, whom I started climbing with in my college years, raised chinchillas and hunted uranium with, and Butch Pritchett, who climbed all the Colorado 14ers with us Smiths over the years. And, thanks go to my second wife Peggy (deceased), who also topped them all.

I appreciate being part of the square dance and round dance world. That community has been an important part of my life for more than seventy years. People who square and round dance are a special breed—friendly, honest, dependable and caring. If you are one of them, you know what I mean.

Thanks also to the climbers we crossed paths with over the years with whom we share memories.

Preface

In 1932, I experienced a traumatic childhood injury just before I turned age 4, that strongly affected my outlook on life. This book, *The Bark of the Cony*, tells about many life adventures and emphasizes a major life philosophy of mine, "Not If, But How." It pretty much quits after 1969 when my four sons and I finished climbing all of the 14,000-foot mountains, ("14ers"), in the contiguous United States for the first time. There is some mention in the book of us climbing all the 14ers a second time in the summer of 1974. There is also reference to "The Climbing Smiths School of Mountaineering," which we offered in the summers from 1971 through 1978. Our climbing school motto was "Not If, But How."

The thought of writing this book in the first place started in 1969, and I wrote nine rough-draft chapters. The original title was to be "Not If, But How," but in 1974 I decided to call the book *The Bark of the Cony*. Unfortunately, due to the challenges and priorities of day to day life, the book never happened. Now, forty-six years later, with the help of my sons, the book is finished.

The Foreword was written in October 1974 by Frank Haraway, a Sports Writer for *The Denver Post*, and contains references to those rough-draft chapters. How could that be?

Frank Haraway and my sister, Dorothy Burkhardt, both lived in the Polo Club apartments in Denver. Dorothy was a great promoter for us and she shared those rough-draft chapters with him in 1974. Earlier than that, in 1945, he wrote an article about me when I was playing baseball at East High School in Denver. That story can be found in Appendix 1. In that article his description of my right hand was wrong but he later corrected it in the Foreword he wrote for this book.

I'm not proud of my name. Smith is okay but there have been too many George Smiths. Hence my pen name, G. Nash Smith, which I use when I write poems, stories, and what I call, "Thought Cards," some of which are in this book. My wife, Marilou, and I had four sons over seven years. Because I didn't like a common front name to go with Smith, the boys had to have a first name I had never heard used as a first name. As a result, there is Flint K, Quade B, Cody J, and Tyle A Smith. The middle name is just an initial and if someone puts a period after the initial the name is misspelled. I am proud of my boys and I am proud of their names.

I hope you find *The Bark of the Cony* to be entertaining, educational, inspiring, and that it gives you a laugh, a lift, and the confidence to raise your bar of achievement. Maybe you will find that you can do more than you thought possible.

Foreword

FRANK HARAWAY, 1974

Logically, perhaps, the words you are about to read should have been written by a person who has lived the challenge, the toil, the thrills and the rewards of mountain climbing. For this book is the first-person story of a gutty guy named George Smith and his successes in this most demanding of all outdoor sports.

I know nothing about mountain climbing except what I have seen in a few movies. But in the field of sports writing, which I have done for the last 37 years, you get to know people of all kinds—good, bad, indifferent, motivated, and unmotivated. One of the most fascinating people it has been my pleasure to know on my trail is George Smith.

I had heard of George before I knew him. His father, Tupper Smith, and my father, Bill Haraway, were close friends and business acquaintances. I heard my dad mention that Tupper Smith had a son named George who had had a most unfortunate accident that had rendered his right arm virtually useless.

Next time I heard of George Smith was some 15 years later while covering high school sports for The Denver Post. Denver East High School had an outfielder who played with one arm, batted one-handed (at a +.300 average), and made a significant contribution to the success of his team. That boy was George Smith.

Smith's accident left him with 3 semi-stiff fingers, no thumb or index finger, an elbow frozen at a right angle with a 30° mobility factor and zero wrist action.

The thought of competing successfully in such sports as baseball, basketball, football and mountain climbing with such a handicap would not have been contemplated by any normal boy. But George Smith was not an ordinary boy in any sense of the word.

He was only 4 years old at the time of his mishap and in the formative years immediately ahead, he developed the determined philosophy which has enabled him to conquer physical problems that would have defied most "normal" persons.

He refused to consider his mutilated arm as a handicap. Indeed, he transformed it into a philosophical asset which was to be the driving force in his life.

"I learned I could do anything I wanted to do," George writes in an early chapter in this fascinating book. "...That handicap was to give birth to a driving force within me that would change my life and affect the lives of many others... My handicap would be transformed into an asset, as far as my thinking was concerned. I learned to do things that two-armed people did, and because of it, I was looked upon as being above normal."

As Smith writes in this book, "a pattern developed. I had positive-thinking people working to convince me that I could do as well as anyone with two arms, and once I was convinced that I could, then I wanted to do even better. It became a habit, a compulsion, a driving force that compelled me to do my best at whatever it was. If my best wasn't good enough, okay; but I had to give it a go."

If one paragraph in the author's own words could express George Smith's adult motivation, it would be this one: "The mountains are my religion. I belong to the First Church of the Great Outdoors. The easiest way for me to escape from the monetarily American way of life is to climb to the top of a mountain. My thoughts, decisions, and problems are sifted out for me in this clean air. Big problems become little, and little problems evaporate. I return home pleasantly exhausted but with new-found strength and direction with which to meet my world head-on."

It is not surprising that the combination of Smith's love of the mountains and his fierce competitive spirit would lead him in the direction of mountain climbing. And in true George Smith fashion, it meant that he would have to tackle the mightiest peaks--not just a few of them but all 67 of the 14,000+ foot peaks in the United States, and in typical George Smith fashion, nothing would do but to conquer the 67 peaks... not once in a lifetime but twice up to this writing.

The story of George Smith really is the story of the George Smith family. George and his wife Marilou have four sons to whom they gave the distinctive names of Flint, Quade, Cody, and Tyle. And, almost as soon as they were able to walk without a wobble, each became a member of the Smith family mountain climbing team.

The pages you are about to read offer a wealth of inspiration, philosophy, and heart-warming accomplishment and love of family.

—Frank Haraway, October, 1974

Prelude

How Far is Far?

It was early afternoon on September 1, 1969 when the following conversation took place:

"What are you, a Boy Scout troop?"

"No Sir, we are a family. These four boys are brothers."

"How far ya goin'?"

"To the top."

"Wow! Ya got a long way to go."

And after taking a picture for us, the old man whose curiosity we had aroused headed down the asphalt path towards the lodge at Paradise at the base of Mount Rainier, in the state of Washington (see photo 1).

That old man's reference to "Ya got a long way to go," has two sides to it. True, to reach the summit of Mount Rainier, we still had 9,000 feet of elevation to gain and eighteen miles round trip to hike, which to him was a long way. But not to us five Smith kids, considering in our journey to get here we had already hiked over 600 miles, and gained over 230,000 feet in elevation. It depends on which side of a statement you are on.

But, why were we standing here about to climb Mount Rainier in the first place? I am glad you asked. To answer that, however, we have to start at the beginning, my beginning. It's not a short story, so pull up a chair and make yourself comfortable.

Photo 1 – Mount Rainier from the Paradise parking lot (from left: Flint, Quade, Cody, Tyle, and George) day 23 from home, September 1, 1969

Chapter 1

CAR POOL

I was born in 1928 and was the youngest of five children. I had two older sisters, Kay and Dorothy, and two older brothers, Tupper and Keene, in that order. Kay was 10 years older than me. In 1932 I was the only one in my family not old enough to be in school. Four families in the block had a car-pool system and it was the next-door-neighbor's week to drive the neighborhood kids to and from Stevens Elementary School, morning, noon, and late afternoon. He had a big black four-door Studebaker that he parked on the left side of his two-car garage. Back in those days, a two-car garage had a four-by-four center post. The wooden doors on each side slid sideways on their own overhead track. Only one side of the garage could be open at a time.

In early May, one month before my fourth birthday, my right arm was severely injured. The fateful day was May 9th and it was noontime. My parents were in Colorado Springs attending a business convention. My brothers and sister Dorothy were due to be picked up at school. I was across the alley in the Perkins' back yard (without permission), playing on a tree swing. Agnes, our maid, was the only one around, and she was in our house.

When I heard the neighbor start his car I decided I wanted to ride to school with him to pick up the car-pool kids, but he didn't know it. I got off of the swing, ran across the alley through his backyard and into his garage. I jumped on the passenger-side running board as he was backing out. The car was already about a third of the way out of the garage and the neighbor was looking to his left.

Unfortunately, the left-side garage door had not been completely opened. It lacked about sixteen inches of being flush with the four-by-four center post. There was enough room for him to back out straight but there was not much clearance on the right side of the vehicle. While the car was backing, at the very moment I opened the front passenger door with my right hand, the car door hit the protruding garage door with my arm wedged in between. I screamed. "Crack," the garage door broke off and my arm immediately became a giant blood blister. He stopped the car and I was taken to Children's Hospital. My parents were summoned home. To make a long story short, according to the doctors, I was lucky they were able to save any of my right arm from the shoulder down. Gangrene set in. My thumb and forefinger were amputated. My right hand looked more like a claw than a hand. I was left with a withered arm and three dwarfed, semi-stiff fingers. My elbow was frozen at a right angle, and I had thirty-degree flex action in my elbow and zero wrist action.

Needless to say, the hospital and doctor bills were staggering. My folks didn't have any Blue Cross-type insurance plan. They tightened their belts and dug in. Agnes, the maid, had to be let go. I don't know how they did it, but I do know the impressions I carried with me into my teenage years had nothing to do with money or the hardships my accident had caused them. Instead, what I gained from my upbringing was the desire to pull my own weight and the self-confidence that I could. I became determined to do as well as anyone with two arms. I actually resented someone offering me help or assistance when I sensed it was done out of pity. I needed to figure out my own way to do something in order to keep up with the others, but with time to think and experiment, I learned how to compete equally.

A heartbreaking tragedy with the "reward" of being "handicapped" for the rest of my life, you say? No, not really. As stated in the Prelude, it depends on which side of a statement you are on. That so called "handicap" became a driving force within me that would change how I would live my life and consequently affect the lives of many others.

> *"Everyone has a handicap of some sort, some you can see*
> *and some you can't."*
> **G. NASH SMITH**

Photo 2 – Me at age 3, 1931, before my injury

Photo 3 – My family before my injury (from left: Kay, Tupper, me (age 3), Mom, Dorothy, and Keene), circa 1931

Chapter 2

I Had No Shoes

When I got home from the hospital, the mood was all positive. My family offered nothing but encouragement. Therapy treatments at the hospital continued. My mom enrolled me in Christian Science Sunday School, which stressed positive thinking. I attended regularly for quite a while.

If I did something deemed wrong now and then, I was treated the same as my siblings. We got a swat on the behind. And, if what we did was bad enough, the swat was with a switch we got to pick out ourselves from a fallen cherry tree branch in the backyard.

My mom was the more influential of my parents, and it was through her efforts that I learned one must never cease working towards a worthwhile goal. She stressed something good could come from something bad. Once she left a note card in a place where I would be sure to find it that read, "I had no shoes and complained until I met a man who had no feet." That message is still with me and became one of the principles of my life's formula. As I look back, if I was destined to get my arm mangled, I'm glad it happened to me when I was young and had no skills. Had I been an adult when this happened, I'm sure the transformation from being right-handed to left-handed would've been much harder.

My sisters, Kay and Dorothy, were always positive and showed genuine interest in my progress. They were excited when I accomplished something new, like learning to tie my shoes. I learned how to do that with the help of a friend and classmate, Bobby Binstock, who lived on the next block.

My brothers, Tupper and Keene, without knowing it, helped me in a way no one else could. They showed no sympathy and wouldn't let me use my arm as a handicap. The three of us would scuffle a lot and usually it was two against one, and more often than not I was the one. If I said things like, "Ouch, my arm," or "Get off me," or, "Let go, my arm," they didn't change what they were doing.

So, I learned I couldn't use my injury as an excuse. I have my brothers to thank for that (see photo 5). In retrospect, that helped put me over the hump. Another way my brothers influenced me was through their success in sports, which I tried hard to equal. We played a lot of sports.

Learning to catch and hit a baseball one-handed gave me a real boost of confidence. A teammate and I could play catch with each other as fast as the two guys next to us. I would catch the ball in a glove on my left hand, toss the ball into the air, remove the glove by tucking it in the pit of my right arm, re-catch the ball with my left hand, and complete the throw. I batted left-handed, my right hand was used only to steady my grip on the bat. I couldn't hit for power but if I watched the ball hit the bat like one is supposed to, I produced a lot of singles, a few doubles, and once in a while a triple. Also, I got pretty good at football, basketball, ping-pong, badminton, putt-putt golf, and horseshoes. I even wrestled and boxed in grade school and junior high. If someone said I couldn't accomplish a certain challenge, I would secretly set out to prove them wrong. We enjoyed a great family bond, and it was what they did and didn't do in regard to me that leaves me forever in their debt.

So, with the help of positive-thinking people, a pattern developed. During the ten years after my accident, I learned that I could usually do as well as anyone with two arms, and once I learned I could, I challenged myself to do my best at whatever it was. I didn't like to lose at anything. My "handicap" was transformed into an asset, as far as my thinking was concerned. If I accomplished equally with the guy with two arms, I got more credit than he did, but from my point of view I was just doing an equal share.

If I had wanted to accept it, my standard of achievement could have been lowered and still sanctioned as being okay by others; but I didn't want that type of praise. In retrospect, during the early years after my injury I was too young to have many opinions about anything. The only opinion I remember I had was that I liked ice cream. But because of the positive direction I received during those formative years of my life when it counted most, I learned not to seek favoritism for my injury. I came to accept that I was normal in an abnormal way.

"It doesn't take much talent to become a parent, but it takes a whole lot of talent to be a parent."
G. NASH SMITH

Photo 4 – Family reunion, circa 1933: I am front row right, hiding my injured hand

Photo 5 – From left: Me, brothers Keene and Tupper, ages approximately 6, 8, 10, circa 1934

Chapter 3

Stops Along the Way

Pop Stand

During the summers of 1936, 1937 and 1938, my brothers and I had a pop stand that was a block and a half from our home, on a vacant lot at the corner of 8th Avenue and Steele Street. At that time traffic on 8th Avenue went both directions.

I don't know how or why this venture came about. Maybe our folks just thought it would be a good learning experience and gave us something to do to keep busy.

I was age 8. Brother Keene was 10 and Brother Tupper was 12 when, in 1936, my Dad had a carpenter friend, Mr. Erickson, build us a pop stand. It was four feet on the front and back and eight feet on the sides and six feet high. The framework was two-inch by four-inch lumber. There was no floor. On the sides and front end was a quarter-inch plywood forty inches high starting at ground level. The back end was open for us to enter and bring in the pop and pop cooler (which I still have). The roof was an orange canvas lid my mom had made that overhung a foot on all four sides. White tassels were added every six inches. There was open air from the side walls to the canvas. A one-foot counter was at the front end. All the wood was painted a light blue.

To get the pop back and forth between home and the pop stand each day we used a three-foot by three-foot wooden platform that rolled on furniture casters. It was pulled by a rope that was attached to the two front corners. Both Tupper and Keene were involved. Usually Tupper, my oldest brother, was the puller. He pulled that platform down the street, while Keene watched for traffic. I used the sidewalk.

We were open daily from 9 a.m. to 3 p.m., closed on Sunday. I was usually the only one on duty. My brothers had baseball practice. My pay was one bottle of pop per day.

We were the only pop stand in Denver that pop companies delivered to. We sold Coca-Cola, 7Up and assorted flavors from Duffy's Delicious Drinks. Maddox Ice Company gave us a cardboard sign to hang out when we needed another twenty-five-pound block of ice. The ice and pop was kept in the 7Up cooler. It was a metal rectangle thirty-one inches by twenty-two inches, three feet tall, painted dark blue. The top half was enclosed and held ice and pop and the bottom half was open and held cases of pop, empty or full. It had wheels that didn't roll good in the dirt (see photo 6).

Photo 6 – Pop cooler, circa 1936

Our sales pitch was, "We have ice cold Coca-Cola, Root Beer, Cherry, Orange, Lemon/Lime, Strawberry, Grape, 7Up, Cream Soda, and Double Duck."

A case of twenty-four bottles cost us $1.30 with a credit of fifty cents when we returned a case of empties. We sold pop for five cents each. Our profit per case was forty cents and we sold an average of two cases per day.

Most of our customers were in trucks or cars that stopped, not many were on foot. The pop was consumed on-site because we needed to keep the empties. Our most frequent customer was a kid about my age who lived four blocks away on 6th and Milwaukee. I didn't know him because we went to different schools. He had to be a rich kid to spend five cents as often as he did. Sometimes he didn't have a nickel but we extended credit.

His credit was good. His name was Ed Tynan. He ended up with two first-rate auto dealerships on Havana Street, Volkswagen and Nissan, a mile from where I live in Aurora. Small world, huh?

Our pop stand couldn't happen today without a license from the city. The pop stand and pop cooler sat on the corner all summer and no vandalism took place. Those were the good old days.

"If you are happy doing what you are
doing then you are a success."
G. Nash Smith

Denver Athletic Club (DAC)

The Denver Athletic Club (DAC) was a big part of my growing-up years. My Dad was a member all of his adult life and even served on the Board a time or two. My Dad went to the DAC every Saturday and he would play billiards. I tagged along. In the mornings I practiced basketball. There was a woodworking shop where I spent some time. Bud Preisser was the shop manager. His brother, Chet, gave me some square dance caller leads when I began calling square dances in the early 1950s. A good friend of my Dad, Jerry Campbell, helped me learn to swim at the DAC.

Another person who influenced me in my early days was Albert "Bo" Place. He was a quality guy. Bo was my football and baseball coach when I played for the DAC in the Young American League (YAL) from ages 8 through 14. He had been a champion wrestler in high school and college and was a fierce competitor. I consider myself fortunate that he was my coach. He inspired me and helped me improve my sporting skills. During the six years I played football and baseball for the DAC they had only two championship teams. They were in football, and I was on both of them. From these experiences I gained athletic skills and confidence.

One of my Dad's friends, Mr. Moser of Niles & Moser cigar fame, took a liking to me and he would give me a quarter regularly. After basketball I would go to Rockybilt Hamburgers that was at the alley on the same block as the DAC. I would buy two hamburgers for five cents each and a five-cent Pepsi for lunch. Then I would walk north two blocks to 16th Street and go to a movie at the Denver Theater for ten cents, then back to the DAC to ride home with my Dad. My sister, Kay, was often the cashier on duty at the theater but I still paid ten cents.

I coached the DAC Junior A football team in the fall all three of my high school years.

Chickens

When I was 13 to 15 years old we had a pair of Black Cochin Bantam chickens. Cleo was the female and Pinocchio was the male. I think it was my Mom's idea of a way to teach me about the "birds and the bees." The chickens were about two-thirds the size of normal chickens and had black feathers at their ankles. We had a small chicken coop and chicken house near the alley between the ashpit and the two-car garage next door (where I got my arm hurt). In the coop was a small chicken house big enough for maybe eight chickens to roost.

We weren't in the chicken-raising business so we never had many chicks. Bantam eggs are small in size but taste good. It was against the law to have chickens in Denver because of their crowing. Pinocchio could crow and so could Tuffy, one of the chicks that became my favorite.

What about the crowing, you ask? No problem. At about 5 p.m. each day, Cleo, Pinocchio and Tuffy would be at the back door of the house. I would open the screen door and into the house they would come. They would turn left and hop down nine basement steps, go across the laundry room and across the maid's room (where Agnes was living when I hurt my arm) to a closet by the outside wall. In the closet was a one-inch-square by thirty-inch-long wooden stick for them to roost on. And they would hop up onto it. There was crowing but it was muffled. We never got a citation.

In the morning at about seven o'clock, someone, usually my Mom, would open the closet door and out they would come. When they got to the steps they hopped up to the screen door that was being held open for them. Then they waddled thirty-five feet down the eighteen-inch cement walk to their pen where there was a treat for them. One year I entered three chickens in competition at the annual Stock Show held each January and won a third-place ribbon.

Tuffy was my favorite. He was unique. I took him on a couple of Boy Scout campouts. On one of them at Congress Park, he got his picture in the newspaper. On another one it was a father/son campout at Genesee. It was late afternoon, about five o'clock, and he was missing. I couldn't find him. Help! What happened? Where is he? Did some animal get him? It turns out he had found a place to roost underneath one of the cars. The real kicker with Tuffy was his bike riding. I had a two-wheel Iver Johnson bike and I attached a one-inch-square by eighteen-inch wooden stick across the handlebars. I would put Tuffy on that stick and we would go for a short ride up and down our block. Tuffy was my "hood ornament." He was a little wobbly but never fell off. What a fun chicken he was.

Dancing

I started square dancing in 1938 when I was in 5th grade at Stevens Elementary School at 12th and Columbine Street. Chet Preisser was the leader. It was sort of a cotillion-type of group that danced two Fridays a month at the Greenleaf Lodge at 4th and Saint Paul Street. What I remember most was that some of the girls didn't like to touch my right hand as we danced.

At that time the Denver Recreation Department offered a summer square dance program. I participated a couple of summers at Cheesman Park. My partner was Margaret Sherlock. In junior high I would ride my bike once a week after school from Aaron Gove to 23rd and Fairfax for dance lessons at Martha Frye Dance Studio. My partner was Emmy Lou Peters.

Three times a week I would ride my bike to the football/basketball field at City Park near the Museum of Natural History building for football/baseball practice with DAC. It was considered to be a strange and incompatible combination of activities to play sports and of all things dance, too. I was a weird kid.

Haircuts

I was the fraternity house barber in college. I had a few loyal customers. My room was the shop and the cost was twenty-five cents.

I cut my Dad's hair in the basement of the house on Saint Paul Street in the late stages of his life. He died in 1959 at age 67, the same year Tyle was born.

I cut hair for my boys early on. Quade was age 14 when he got his first store-bought haircut.

Other Stops Along the Way

We have talked about three major subjects as I was growing up. But there were a lot of short, one-time entries. While at Aaron Gove Junior High School, I shoveled snow off my neighbors' walks in the winter for $1 and cut their lawns in the summer for $1. I also offered to paint house numbers on the concrete steps in front of houses using numeric stencils. Sumner Downing, a school chum, and I set pins at the Park Hill Bowling Alley. It was a life-threatening job that paid five cents a line. We had to really watch out for flying bowling pins.

In the 1944 summer, Sumner Downing and I both worked at Burkhardt Steel & Iron Works. We removed welding spurs off of really big sheets of iron that had something to do with battleships and World War II.

In the summer of 1945, I worked at the Park Hill Golf Course moving hoses to water the greens. My salary was $150 per month.

At Christmastime during my high school years, I sold Christmas wreaths. I took over that business from my brother, Tupper, when he went to college. We ordered wreaths from Barteldes Seed Company and hung them in the two-car garage at our house. The garage rafters were full. We sold about sixty wreaths every Christmas. The most popular wreath was twelve inches and cost eighty-five cents.

On a different subject, my first store-bought haircut cost twenty-five cents. The shop was on 6th Avenue and St. Paul Street. Claude Sarchet was the barber. The streetcar ran on 6th Avenue. The cost of a ride was ten cents or buy three tokens for a quarter. The Bonita Drug Store, run by George Moore, was on the corner of 6th Avenue and St. Paul Street. There was a Piggly Wiggly Food Market a block west. Lloyd King of King Soopers-to-be fame, lived two houses south of us. But I digress....

As I was growing up, part-time jobs were hard to come by and I was glad to find work where I could.

Chapter 4

Compared to What?

From the summit of a tall mountain you can see many things very clearly. If you would look back at the route you took to get to the top, you would see some things that you didn't notice on the way up.

As fate would have it, in 1943 I became the acting troop leader of Boy Scout Troop 1, because I was an Eagle Scout and the oldest boy by a few months. Even though I was just 15 years old, I assumed the leadership responsibilities because our Scoutmaster, Bob Shurtleff, had been called to serve in World War II.

Each summer, some Troop 1 scouts would go to Camp Tahosa, a Boy Scout camp near Ward, Colorado. In 1944 we spent a two-week session there. Upon learning of our circumstance, one woman remarked, "How dreadful, those poor little boys without a Scoutmaster!" when she heard we were the only troop in camp without an adult leader.

It was a valid point on the surface but unnecessary in this situation. We had a going bunch of tough little kids, and to be without an adult leader didn't hamper our approach. Whether we were at camp or in town, our program called for winning no matter the subject. Whether the contest was scout advancement, fire building, water boiling, knot tying, horseshoes, softball, pulling a chariot, pyramid building, wall scaling, playing Capture the Flag, or picking up trash, our goal was to win.

Each year at Camp Tahosa our troop made a point to occupy the permanent campsite that was the furthest from the building complex and assembly area. In spite of the distance handicap of about a half-mile versus 400 feet for the closest unit, we enjoyed consistently being the first unit with total membership present when assembly was required. We were first to line up for daily inspection near the mess hall. A little running never hurt anybody. We had a fantastic crew that thrived on winning. Four years in a row we won the award for being the best troop in camp during our two-week stay. We did it without an adult to lead us. "Poor little boys," indeed!

The camp director, Dave Boardman, granted us permission to be our own unit, since we had earned his trust and respect by proving ourselves to be reliable at camp without an adult leader. Camp Tahosa's elevation is 9,000 feet. During each week of camp, on a certain day every boy was required to go on a hike of some kind. Some kids hiked to Fresno Pond, and more kept going uphill on the trail to Brainard Lake, and that's what our troop did.

We chose to be the last group to leave camp. We set a pace and kept it up. Hup, two, three, four. Hup, two, three, four. In about a half hour we caught up with the stragglers, and in an hour we had passed all there were to pass.

It was around noon when the hike counselor lined up everyone who had hiked to Brainard Lake to explain the options for the remainder of the day, one of which was hiking further to Lake Isabelle, elevation 10,868 feet, to join an exclusive club called the Alpine Dippers. To claim membership in the Alpine Dippers one had to completely submerge in a lake above 10,000 feet in elevation. The membership was good for one year. He announced, "All scouts not going to Lake Isabelle to join the Alpine Dippers fall out."

So help me, we had not discussed or pre-arranged among ourselves what we would do individually or as a group in regard to the Alpine Dippers. I watched our kids looking from side to side without moving their heads to see who was going to fall out. At least half of the line fell out but not a single one of our boys flinched. Twenty-four scouts, counting the hike counselor, elected to go the three extra miles to Lake Isabelle, and twenty-one of them were from our troop, Troop 1, Capitol Heights District, Denver, Colorado. That was a really proud moment for me!

We joined the Alpine Dippers that afternoon in water that was partially covered with ice and so cold that we found ourselves gasping for air. A unique experience for sure.

On our way back to the main camp, when we got to Fresno Pond there were two scouts near the shoreline wading and splashing about. I asked, "How's the water?" "It's coooold!" came the reply. Compared to Lake Isabelle, Fresno Pond was shallow and much lower in elevation and didn't have any ice, the water temperature was bound to be warmer.

If you were to ask those two boys for their definition of cold water, they would no doubt have said Fresno Pond. Based on their experience that day, they were being truthful. To them the water had been really cold.

Baloney! Those two kids didn't have the slightest idea of what it was like to experience cold water. Hadn't I been in a glacier-fed lake at nearly 11,000 feet? I knew a lot more about being in cold water than they did. Yet, and here's the point: I realized that there could be somebody else who had been in colder water than I had been in and who could truthfully tell me that I didn't have the slightest idea what it was like to be in really cold water.

Thus, that Alpine Dippers experience hatched for me another major life principle that I call, "Compared to What?" At any given moment of discomfort there is another level worse, and possibly another after that. Whatever it is that you are experiencing—pain, hunger, cold, wetness, heat, fatigue, thirst—it could be worse. You can work a little harder; you can go a little further; you can stand a little more of whatever it is. Complaining doesn't solve a thing. Accept the discomfort as part of the day's work and spend your energy trying to stay the course. Many people are programmed to quit early. Try not to be one of them. The odds are your situation could be worse. Hang in there.

Chapter 5

The Bark of the Cony

"Hey, Warren! Let's go climb Longs Peak."

Warren was Warren Pulis, of Vail, Colorado. He and I became close friends during our years attending Colorado A & M (Agriculture and Mechanic Arts) College in Fort Collins, Colorado. My first year started in the fall of 1946 and I graduated in June of 1950. Warren was a year behind me and we were Sigma Alpha Epsilon (SAE) fraternity brothers. We were both private people possessing strong personal convictions. We shared many like interests and were good competition for each other in horseshoes and ping-pong. We had a similar sense of humor, and developed a complete repertoire of humorous actions and sayings that most people didn't find to be as funny as we did because they hadn't been in on the origin of that particular bit of humor. Others around us would laugh, too, but many times they would be laughing at the two of us laughing at each other.

Ours is one of those rare friendships that shows up only two or three times in a lifetime, and in some cases, never. We can begin right where we left off no matter how much time has elapsed between visits. Time stands still for us. At school we roomed, studied, camped, and in general, messed around together. We worked up a guitar comedy act that was good enough to be used in the talent exchange program with other colleges in the state at that time. Yes, I learned to play the guitar in spite of my right-arm "handicap." Bob Swerer, one of my fraternity sons and the lead singer in his professional group called the "Sons of the Rockies," made a leather strap with a metal pick for me that I attached to my right hand. He taught me how to play chords but I couldn't do anything fancy (see photo 7). Warren and I planned how we would be in business together when we were out of college. Neither of us learned to smoke or drink, simply because it didn't make sense. Whatever we did had to make sense to us no matter what the rest of the world did or didn't do.

During the summers while in college, I worked for Armour & Company, Swift & Company, and the Denver Union Stockyards Company.

My Dad got me that job since I was going to be a rancher. My college degree was to be in Animal Husbandry.

To earn some spending money in college, Warren and I ran a really tasty hamburger concession in the annex building next door to the main SAE fraternity house. Five nights a week and sometimes six, we would cook up twenty-five deluxe hamburgers on our jointly owned Coleman camp stove and sell them to fraternity brothers for twenty-five cents each. We managed seven hamburgers to a pound of meat and got twelve slices out of a three-inch tomato.

On September 1, 1948, Warren and I climbed Longs Peak, near Estes Park (see photos 8, 9). I'm not really sure why we did it other than it was something new for us to do. We climbed the Keyhole route, summited and proudly signed the register. We headed down and when we got below timberline, took a break, then returned to the car. Climbing a mountain was hard work, not that much fun, and I was not sure I wanted to do it again. At the time, I didn't realize the lasting effect this climb would have on my life.

During the year that followed, a lot of soul-searching took place. The pieces of my personal identity puzzle began to surface. The memories of the discomforts and unpleasantries of that first climb had settled to the bottom. I still remembered the physical parts of the climb were strenuous, but taking their place were thoughts of the solitude we experienced and the fantastic views that were ours to enjoy during the climb. I became impressed with the discovery of how simple life was in a complicated, good way.

So, a year later, on September 4 and 5, 1949, we climbed Mounts Elbert and Massive and the result was different. It turned out those mountains were fun versus last year's climb of Longs Peak. Lesson learned: one needs to summit at least a second mountain before deciding if climbing is for you, because on the first climb, neither your mind nor body knows what to expect.

The climbs of Elbert and Massive were fun, but I couldn't let go of my Longs Peak experience. A realization occurred as to just how that climb had affected my approach to life. That was a "yeah," "boo" climb and the "yeah" took a while to show up. Actually, it turns out there was a lot more "yeah" than "boo." How so? Well the "boo" was the hard work that it took to do fifteen miles with a gain of 5,100 feet of elevation. Which was really no fun. But the "yeah" was the by-product of being in the out-of-doors, the wilderness, being away from civilization. It took the second and third climbs for me to realize the value of my experience climbing Longs Peak.

True, I was in college to get book-learned, and yet, as I looked back to our climb of Longs Peak in 1948, I remembered the awkward sensation of being extremely ignorant during our break below timberline. Warren and I had been trespassers badly outnumbered and completely surrounded by the little creatures of timberline, a serene community that is a hubbub of action as well as a mecca for refreshing, bigger-than-life beauty. I realized I knew zilch about the intricate makeup of nature's delicate world, the sights, the sounds, the smells, the systems of plants and animals and their effect on one another.

I remember I was leaning against a boulder and thinking how neat it was out there all by ourselves. Then a chain of events took place that I will never forget. I heard a cony bark a warning to the rest of his clan, telling them an outsider was present (see photo 10). That sound flushed a bevy of little birds that quickly reestablished themselves on some stubby, low-growing evergreen. One bird became silhouetted by a slow-moving, fluffy white cloud. The bird cocked his head to one side and swooped to the ground where he snagged a multi-colored bug whose time had come. A warm, fresh-smelling breeze splashed across the faces of the many varieties of miniature flowers that were standing on their tiptoes, reaching towards the crisp blue sky.

Flit, flit, flit, went a butterfly that was flying as if he'd been drinking. A bee stuck his nose in some flower's business. A pesky housefly, a long way from anybody's house, somehow didn't seem so pesky. Thinking back on that climb I would come to vow that even though I wasn't smart enough to understand the complexities of the master plan, I would respect it to the smallest ant.

The mountains became my religion. I belong to the First Church of the Great Outdoors. The easiest way for me to escape from the monetarily motivated American way of life is to climb to the top of a mountain. My thoughts, decisions, and problems are sifted out for me in the clean air. Big problems become little, and little problems evaporate. I return home pleasantly exhausted but with newfound strength and direction with which to meet my world head-on.

I feel so grateful to have found the mountains. It's like being willed a fortune. I realized I was wealthy. No money, but I was wealthy, and I knew it. I was a non-monetary millionaire. I had crystallized one more principle by which to live my life. Every time I hear a cony bark, I am reminded of the joy of existing.

"I don't know where I am going but I'm a lot
further than I was."
G. NASH SMITH

Photo 7 – Warren Pulis and Bob Swerer, my SAE Fraternity Son at Colorado A & M 1948

Photo 8 – Longs Peak, my first 14er, with Warren Pulis September 1, 1948

Photo 9 – Horse shelter, Longs Peak boulder field

Photo 10 – Cony or Pika, lives in mountainous areas at high elevation, adult length 6-9 inches, istock photo of Pika by Frank Fichtmüller

WHAT'S PRETTY

I'll tell you what's pretty.
The view of the world from a high mountaintop,
A lush meadow of wild flowers dancing
An orange colored sky at the end of a day,
The sun getting up in the morning.

Ducks on a pond, the hoot of an owl,
The sound of katydids singing.

A sky full of stars on a moonlit night,
A mountain stream gently cascading.

A fawn with its' mother who stands at alert,
Colts that bolt for no reason.

Golden wheat fields swaying in the autumn breeze,
Geese flying south for the season.

The sound of dead silence, then a coyote's howl,
The sound of wind through timbers,
The aspen leaves in the fall of the year,
The snow covered peaks in the winter.
That's pretty.

But if you take time to reflect on the beauty around us,
The aspects of nature and how they all fit,
You can't help but marvel how it all has purpose,
We are each a thread in God's quilt.

G. NASH SMITH

Chapter 6

GAME GIRL

The summer of 1948 I worked for Crocker & Ryan Consulting Engineers as a soil tester. The Valley Highway (I-25) was being developed. Ken Vail was my boss. His dad, Charles Vail, was the Chief Engineer of the Colorado Department of Highways at that time. He was who Vail Pass was named after. I worked there until the start of my junior year.

My friend Warren and I were members of the Aggie Haylofters Square Dance Club at Colorado A & M. At a dance early that fall, he and I were sizing up the new crop of freshman girls in attendance. I saw this cute redhead and decided to ask her for a dance. Her name was Marilou Milano. Before I could introduce myself, she startled me by already knowing my name. Since then our life has been one startle after another. As it turned out, she had also attended East High School in Denver and knew of me because I had been Senior Class President.

We dated in college (see photo 11) and enjoyed outdoor activities together. She was a good dancer, smiled a lot, had an exceptionally fine soprano singing voice, and didn't know how to get B's and C's, only A's.

My first summer out of college I worked at Onahu Guest Ranch near Grand Lake as a horse wrangler and entertainer. On Saturday nights I called square dances at the Pine Cone Inn with Bob Swerer and his "Sons of the Rockies" band. Marilou was a waitress nearby at the Corner Cupboard Restaurant (see photos 12-15). She completed four years of college in three years and in August of 1951, soon after her graduation, we were married in Denver.

Almost anyone can, and many do, climb a mountain during their lifetime. After which the key question, as mentioned in the prior chapter, is whether or not that person would be willing to climb a second one. The validity of that question occurred at the expense of Marilou. By that I mean, I didn't break her in correctly. By that I mean, her first climbs weren't too much fun. By that I mean, I doubt that she will ever forget our honeymoon.

For the first week of a two-week honeymoon, we went to Jackson Hole, Wyoming, driving the first vehicle I ever owned, a three-quarter-ton Ford pickup truck that answered to the name of Abraham. In Denver, after stopping at a Frontier gas station to fill up with regular gas costing 18.9 cents a gallon, we headed north. In the truck bed behind the cab was a large plywood box I had built to store stuff. In it was a tent, sleeping bags, a brand-new, long-handled wood axe we bought with some of our wedding money, two heavy Army tarps, two backpacks (one Army and one Boy Scout), an assortment of cooking utensils, and several other camping items of luxury that we thought we couldn't do without, like a foolproof french-fry slicer sold to me by a super saleslady in a Woolworth store. You know, the circus-sideshow type.

We were ready for anything, except for one thing, being able to bathe. We had a round porcelain hand basin and an oval porcelain dishpan but nothing that was big enough to double as a bathtub. On our second day in the Tetons, we went to town and purchased a galvanized-metal laundry tub two feet in diameter and a foot deep for $3.50 to serve that purpose. Whoa there! I'm getting ahead of the story....

It had been close to midnight when we arrived in the Jackson Hole area. As we approached the Tetons, we pulled off the highway on the first two-rutted road we found. It was too late and too dark to set up camp so we parked the truck where it would shield us from the highway. We did not set up a tent. We just rolled the sleeping bags out on unrelated flat spots and proceeded to be lulled to sleep by the sounds of the nearby river. In the morning a noise woke me but at first I did not react. Then, when I heard it a second time I realized it was a man's voice. I slowly widened the sleeping bag zipper and turned to look in the direction of the sound. Zounds! I saw some guy's shoe, with a leg in it, not ten feet from me.

It turns out that we had blindly chosen one of the most spectacular settings in the entire area that night. Where we had pulled off the road the Snake River made a romantic bend between us and the majestic Tetons. Added to that we were surrounded by madly colored wildflowers, plus, as is often the case, there were picturesque clouds rising from Jackson Lake, floating ever so slowly upward to where, at the perfect moment, they would appear to be a ribbon slicing the very top off of Mount Moran.

It was a beautiful picture, and it turned out that's what a lot of other people thought, too. And that is how come that shoe with the leg in it was there when the voice woke me up. For about an hour we were trapped in our sleeping bags as six different sets of tourists came and went, stopping to take pictures. As for the guy with the shoe and the leg, he also had a tripod and was willing to wait for just the right shot. "Bully for him," I reluctantly thought to myself, and then, "Thank God, he finally left." We took a picture, too. Why not? The view was fantastic!

Then we went searching for, and found, a place to camp next to the Snake River that offered more privacy. Unbeknownst to us, the movie, "The Big Sky" was being filmed in the area and it turned out our new location next to the river gave us a front-row seat of the boating scenes being filmed (see photo 16). So, the next day we moved again, lock, stock, and axe handle, to a scrumptious campsite, except for mosquitoes, near Coulter Bay (see photos 17, 18). I tend to be somewhat nomadic. A setting has to be exceptional for me to want to return, and Jackson Hole is one of those areas we would visit again.

A year prior, during October 1950, Warren and I, along with two other guys, fellow Troop 1 Eagle Scouts John Windsor and Freddie Roberts, had climbed a group of three easy 14ers near Fairplay, Colorado, named Democrat, Lincoln and Bross. On Mount Lincoln we had seen an old blacksmith bellows frozen in a snowbank that had been used in the Russia Mine mining operation. A rare find that dated back at least to 1893, the year the Silver Market Crash had changed H.A.W. Tabor's lifestyle. The silver mining industry shut down due to the crash. The thinking was the mining activity would resume the next year but it didn't happen. As a result, buildings and equipment were left to deteriorate or be scavenged.

By the 1950s most of the mines and ghost towns had been scavenged thoroughly but a few items still remained. My first reaction had always been to leave everything as I found it. However, I had also learned that the chances were good the next guy would take said items unless they were too big to handle.

Very cleverly, I had talked Marilou into agreeing to use the second week of our honeymoon to liberate the bellows if still there, to give it a good home. So, after our week in the Tetons we returned to Colorado and Fairplay. From Fairplay we drove six miles to Alma and took the dirt road up Buckskin Gulch that leads to Kite Lake, where we parked Abraham. By the time we headed uphill towards Mount Democrat, each with a full pack, it was late afternoon. Our plan was to spend the night in an abandoned mine building close to the top of Mount Democrat. This would be Marilou's first 14er. When we caught up with the mine building we discovered to our disappointment that it was full of snow. As a result, we spent the night outside the structure on the rocky ground in our sleeping bags.

After breakfast the next morning, August 14, 1951 (see photo 19), we summited Democrat and then navigated the easy ridge across Mount Cameron to Mount Lincoln, but not without incident. Marilou had put her eyeglasses in her boot for safekeeping overnight and before she could return them to her face the next morning, she had put her foot in her boot, breaking a lens. This was not too funny at the time, but later it was deemed humorous. With one eye of no value other than to potentially develop a headache, the day began poorly.

Sure enough, the bellows was still there and with the snow gone it looked to be in fine shape for being 60-plus years of age (see photos 20, 21). I wondered why someone hadn't already carted it off but by the time we had loaded the fifty-six-pound bellows into Abraham the next day, the answer was obvious. It had taken us nine hours over two days to carry the bellows a distance of only two miles as the crow flies. The first mile went reasonably fast because we were able to carry the bellows between us, using the metal rods that protruded from its sides as handles. When we got to where we could see down to Kite Lake and Abraham it looked deceptively close, but the route to get there was much steeper. "We're practically there," I said in a sarcastic W.C. Fields accent.

Now, because what was left was steep and rocky, we had to change our strategy. Marilou could no longer help with the bellows because she had to focus on her own descent. And, because I couldn't carry both the bellows and my pack at the same time, I solved the problem the way I would if I had two cars to drive. I struggled with the bellows a while, and returned to the pack, and carried the pack past the bellows, then returned again to the bellows to carry it past the pack, repeating the overlapping process many times. In the meantime, Marilou was having trouble with depth perception, what with only one good eyeglass plus the approaching darkness. Her lack of mountain experience descending anything, especially a steep slope, caused her to decide to descend seat first. I couldn't talk her out of it.

In an attempt to outsmart our snail's pace, we tried to lighten Marilou's load by sending her backpack downhill on its own. We cinched up her pack as tightly as we could and rolled it towards a rock outcropping, hoping it would stop there. But when the pack got to the outcropping it didn't just stop, it exploded! Bummer! Most of our worldly possessions, including the french-fry slicer, were scattered. So much for that plan. It obviously wasn't a good idea. We retrieved the pack and the scattered items and resumed the overlapping method of descent until, due to darkness, we could no longer continue. So far, we had spent seven hours working with the bellows. We would come back tomorrow to finish the job, which would take another two hours to finally get the bellows, whom we now referred to as "Bill," safely loaded into Abraham.

So, we drove to Fairplay and booked lodging at the historic Hand Hotel. My shins were barked up and the entire seat of Marilou's jeans was gone, and both of us were exhausted. Nobody suspected we were newlyweds. We sure fooled those people.

Photo 11 – Marilou and Rudyard the car with Aggie "A" in background, near Fort Collins 1949

Photo 12 – Performing at Onahu Guest Ranch using guitar pick Bob Swerer made for me summer 1950

Photo 13 – Working as a wrangler, on "Rusty", at Onahu Ranch September 7, 1950

Photo 14 – Feeding a chipmunk at Onahu Ranch 1950

Photo 15 – Calling a Square Dance at the Pinecone Inn 1950

Photo 16 – "Big Sky" movie crew on the Snake River, Teton area, Wyoming 1951

Photo 17 – Jackson Lake, Teton area, Wyoming 1951

Photo 18 – Abraham's box for stuff at our Jackson Lake camp 1951

Photo 19 – Cooking breakfast on Mt. Democrat August 14, 1951

Photo 20 – Marilou with "Bill" the bellows nearby, prior to descent

Photo 21 – Resting up before loading "Bill" the bellows into Abraham

Chapter 7

Two Kinds of Luck

After our episode with Bill the bellows, it was two years before either Marilou or I ventured near another 14er. During that time Warren and I had started Kamer-Nash Chinchillas (see photo 22), and I was delivering sandwiches for Capitol Sandwich Company. My college degree was in Animal Husbandry. I was going to be a rancher but it didn't turn out that way. I had spent some teenage summers helping out and learning the ranching business on an uncle's ranch in northern New Mexico. My granddad on my Mom's side, Jack Zurick, is in the Cowboy Hall of Fame in Oklahoma City. My interest in animals stayed with me. We have always had some form of livestock.

Our first son, Flint, was born in July of 1952. On July 4, 1953, Marilou climbed, and I reclimbed Longs Peak. We had left Flint with her mom, Grandma Milano (Mary). As you probably know, there are two kinds of luck. The climb went well and this trip was in the good luck category. The next weekend we chose to climb Mount Harvard and the other kind of luck showed up.

Mount Harvard is one of the fifteen 14ers in the Sawatch Range, which includes such notables as Mount Elbert, Colorado's highest mountain, Mount Massive, the second-highest, and Mount of the Holy Cross. In 1953, Mount Harvard was listed as being the third-tallest of Colorado's 14ers, and in my opinion, the only one of the fifteen that requires more than plain endurance to climb.

Abraham was still our family auto and his power and high ground clearance came in handy on the road to Lienhart Mine, near Buena Vista, the starting point for the climb. From the mine, Marilou and I began hiking towards a high point in the direction of what we thought was Mount Harvard. When one is inexperienced, the judging of heights can be difficult, especially when it comes to objects "as big as a mountain," such as a mountain itself. What looks like the tallest point from down here is not always the tallest point when you get up there, a fact we learned the hard way. Enter the second kind of luck.

If you've never experienced the sensation of reaching what you thought was the mountaintop only to discover that it was a spur, a false peak, you've missed one of the more unforgettable "thrills" of mountain climbing. That is what happened to us that day. When we got to what we thought was the summit, it wasn't. Someone had moved Mount Harvard (see photo 23). Nuts! There it is, way over there to our right. We trudged the rest of the way to the top, signed our names in the Colorado Mountain Club register, and descended to timberline, where we quit for the day. By then it was pitch dark. We were quite certain that the big open clearing we had seen earlier was near Abraham, but we decided against continuing until we had some help from the morning sun (see photo 24). We huddled all night under a battered tarp, enjoying a lousy night's sleep. In the morning, the clearing we had seen proved to be the correct one. We got back to the car and dined on trail mix. The warm sunshine and soft grassy area felt so good we took a three-hour nap before moving on.

The route we chose to go home would cross the Royal Gorge Bridge, near Cañon City (see photo 25). It is America's highest suspension bridge and spans the Arkansas River. It turned out there was a fee to cross the bridge of ninety cents per person and we only had $1.00. I should have known there would be a cost involved. A problem? No problem. Good ol' Marilou became a stowaway in the box behind the cab that I had built for stuff.

"Hi, Mac, sure is a nice day for a bridge crossing. Beautiful clouds," I commented as I handed the attendant our dollar bill. "Keep the change. Take care." And off we drove, stopping at the first pullout that was out of sight of the toll station so Marilou could get back into the cab. On these two climbs we had experienced good luck, bad luck, plus good luck with a stowaway twist. It felt double good to get back home.

"As you travel life's highway, don't be afraid
to take the alternate route."
G. NASH SMITH

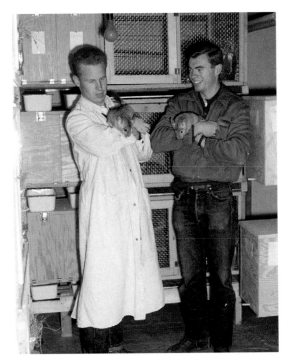

Photo 22 – Kamer-Nash Chinchillas (from left: me, Warren) 1951

Photo 23 – Marilou summiting a false peak. Columbia is in the background June 5, 1953

Photo 24 – Morning light on the way back to Abraham after climbing Mt. Harvard June 6, 1953

Photo 25 – Royal Gorge Toll Bridge June 6, 1953

Chapter 8

North Maroon Peak

In the early 1950s I called square dances and worked for the Denver Recreation Department as a basketball referee. There would be three games a night. My pay was $2 per game, totaling $6. Also, during the summer months on Wednesday nights, I sang and played my guitar at the Brook Forest Inn outside of Evergreen. Chris Mauer was the owner. My charge was $7.

During the summers of 1954 and 1955, Warren and I were hired to hunt for uranium (see photos 26-29). We would prospect from various locations around the state. When it came time to relocate our camp from the Marble area we would be going through Aspen (see photo 30). And because of that, Warren and I decided to take a day off on July 1, 1954, and climb North Maroon Peak. This might be the only chance that summer for us to climb a 14er. After all, we weren't being paid to climb mountains. So far, Warren and I had climbed eight 14ers together, but nothing like North Maroon.

The Maroon Bells are famous for their beauty and for their danger, and are considered to be a couple of the toughest 14ers in Colorado. To climb North Maroon, we would rely on one of my main life philosophies, which is to start out towards your goal and see if you have what it takes to handle the challenges ahead. The route had a lot more straight up than our previous climbs, so we had to pay close attention. The climb required a skill level we hadn't used before. Every once in a while we would stop to take in the scenery (see photo 31). Warren and I were really proud to sign this summit register (see photos 32, 33)! We had some lunch, took a picture, and looked for a different way off the mountain. There had to be a better way than the way we came up.

So, we headed for a couloir that looked promising, but guess what? It wasn't. It was lousy. It narrowed to a chimney that was steep and too tight for us to keep our packs on. I downclimbed about fifteen feet to a ledge. Now it was Warren's turn. Before he started he dropped both packs to me, then downclimbed to me on the ledge. The route opened up. We put our packs back on, got to the valley floor, found the trail and followed it to the car. We got back safely but I have a vivid memory of that hair-raising descent. I think Warren and I made a first descent of that down route. For sure it's not one I would recommend and probably not in anybody's guidebook (see photo 34).

Our next uranium location was south of Fairplay. Over the two summers if we got Geiger counter readings, we would go to the county seat and file a mining claim. We filed several claims but none were ever developed (see Appendix 2).

"Nobody ever did anything the first time without
doing it for the first time."
G. NASH SMITH

Photo 26 – At our uranium camp near Marble 1954

Photo 27 – Geiger counter and pick used for hunting uranium 1954

Photo 28 – Outside the Marble jail camp 1954

Photo 29 – Inside the Marble jail camp 1954

Photo 30 – Looking at the Bells (North Maroon is on the right)

Photo 31 – Rest break on the slopes of North Maroon Peak

Photo 32 – Warren on the summit of North Maroon Peak July 1, 1954

Photo 33 – On the summit of North Maroon Peak July 1, 1954

Photo 34 – Me descending couloir, North Maroon (blurred photo)

Chapter 9

Where Are The Horses?

In January, 1956, our second son, Quade, was born. That is the year I decided I wanted to climb all the Colorado 14ers, which at that time numbered 52. In the eight years since I started with Longs Peak, I added twelve more 14ers. At that rate I would be at least age fifty when I finished, not a swift pace, to be sure. In 1956 I made eight different climbing trips with various people, and at the end of that summer my total was 28 14ers. I was "practically there."

One of those trips was near Lake City with Marilou and her brother, Art Milano. He and I did Handies Peak on Saturday, August 4, from the Silver Creek Trailhead. Marilou and I had intended to climb Redcloud and Sunshine Peaks from the same camp the next day. She and I took a route that was suggested in the 1955 edition of Robert Ormes' book, titled, *Guide to the Colorado Mountains*. We encountered a scree slope while climbing Redcloud Peak and if you've never climbed on scree then you've never climbed with rocks in your boots. Scree is a steep slope of small rocks similar in size to what is common on a schoolyard playground. For every two steps going up we slid back one, becoming both tired and exasperated at the same time, disproving the old adage you can't do two things at once. We made it to the top, emptied the rocks out of our boots, and signed the register. Marilou chose to stay put on Redcloud while I walked the ridge to Sunshine Peak and back again (see photo 35). We then returned to Art at camp, packed up and headed home.

My final trip that summer was with Marilou over Labor Day weekend. The starting point was Hatchers Dude Ranch, which is near Powderhorn, Colorado, about halfway between Gunnison and Lake City. To get within a reasonable hiking distance of San Luis and Stewart Peaks, we rented horses. I had worked with horses in my teenage years on my uncle's cattle ranch in northern New Mexico and I had also worked as a wrangler on the Onahu Guest Ranch near Grand Lake, Colorado, my first summer out of college, so I felt confident.

We rode about thirteen miles to reach the entrance gate at Bonholder Meadows (see photo 36), opened and closed the gate, and then rode another four miles where we found a good spot to make camp and stake the horses. The next morning, after I cooked a hearty chuck-wagon-type breakfast with meat and potatoes, we covered our camping gear with a tarp and rode another three or four miles uphill to the head of the valley and a final group of trees at timberline, where Marilou would remain with the horses while I went climbing.

San Luis Peak was the first of the two, and I made the climb without anything happening worth mentioning. From San Luis to Stewart and back again was a long four miles. During the return from Stewart, the heavy chuck-wagon breakfast was trying to chuck, and I became sicker than a dog. (I wonder how that expression got started?) I visualized Marilou enjoying a carefree afternoon, watching the horses graze and listening to the sounds of an elegant alpine meadow, and probably catching a wink of sleep while I was laboriously making my way back. This was my first climbing experience feeling sick. It was no fun.

When I was on the downhill side of San Luis, I began to feel better and my pace returned to normal. However, because it was getting dark I chose to use a flashlight. Finally, I could see the trees where Marilou and the horses should be.

"Helloooo," I hollered. No answer came back. Maybe I wasn't close enough yet, plus the breeze was against me.

"Helloooo," I repeated.

"Over here," came Marilou's faint reply. I felt relieved.

"Everything okay?"

"Oh, am I glad to see you!" she hugged.

"Where are the horses?"

"They're gone," she sobbed.

"What happened?"

"They got spooked and headed down the trail."

Obviously, I didn't do a good job of staking them. With great disappointment we started hiking back to our camp. We tried to be extra quiet, walking softly and not talking. Maybe the horses hadn't gone back to the meadow, but the odds were they had. I was ninety-five percent sure that's where they'd be unless someone left the gate open. The next morning, we gathered up our stuff and carried everything back to Bonholder Meadows. And guess what? The horses were there off in the distance, near the gate.

There were two fishermen, one near and one far.

We approached the first fisherman and already knowing what the answer would be, I whimsically asked if he had seen any horses. "Yes," he replied, pointing in their direction. "Oh, good, I see them. Thanks." And off we went to retrieve the horses. Then we opened and shut the gate and rode the thirteen miles back to Hatchers. We settled up with the rental fee, and headed home. It was good that the gate was closed. Otherwise, I hate to think how this trip might have ended.

"Always leave the gate like you found it."
G. NASH SMITH

Photo 35 – Marilou on the summit of Redcloud Peak August 5, 1956

Photo 36 – Marilou on horseback in Bonholder Meadows (blurred photo) September 1956

Chapter 10

Problems Must Wait Their Turn

My "hurry up" plan to climb all the 14ers stalled. After climbing fifteen 14ers in 1956, I was only able to add four more during the next five years. Marilou and I were faced with major events and life decisions that prevented me from doing little more than chase after the dollar.

In 1957 I abandoned a salaried job as a property maintenance manager to become a real estate salesman with Monte Carroll & Company, working on commission only. This was in June, about the same time our third son, Cody, was born. In the fall of 1957 we started building our house on a five-acre plot of land in Arapahoe County, east of Denver. A couple of years earlier I had put a down payment on the land. We finished building our home in the spring of 1958 (see photos 37, 38).

I had done the ceramic tile work in our two bathrooms with no prior experience, which was a really memorable challenge for me. As a result, the word tile stuck with me, and with a change of spelling, that became the name of our fourth son, "Tyle," who was born in July of 1959. And guess what? In sixty years I have yet to hear of another "Tyle" (see photo 39). Late in 1960 and early 1961 we built a square dance and private-party facility known as The Outpost on the same five-acre plot of ground (see photos 40-42). This became the home of Bill the bellows. Over the years The Outpost became the most unique square dance hall in all of America and maybe the world.

For us to consider undertaking all this took a great deal of money and nerve. The nerve was ours, but the money wasn't. What we had was good credit, people believing in us enough to loan us money, our willingness to work, and a relentless faith in the method of attacking problems, which the mountains had taught me.

Throughout our marriage Marilou had been steadily employed, either as a dietitian or later as a nutritionist. I sold real estate by day and called square dances by night.

The tougher a situation is, the more I rely on my life philosophies, similar to the way a pilot of an airplane must rely on his instrument panel when he can no longer see due to clouds or bad weather. The value of the philosophies, however, cannot be conveyed by words alone; they must be learned from experience, and the earlier the age, the better.

After my childhood accident and subsequent experiences during my formative years, it was like I was being processed through an extremely hot "blacksmith kiln." I was molded and formed and emerged as an adult with very strong beliefs and a nearly impregnable attitude. Likewise, it could be surmised that I would be a bearcat to live with, unless one was tuned in on the same frequency as me, so as to be able to hear the same drummer. I would not be a good vice president, it should appear obvious that I need to be in charge.

During those years of genuine struggle for us, it developed that I couldn't discuss certain topics with Marilou, namely money and its related subjects; bills, payments, debts and notes due. I would tell her of financial matters in the very same way I would tell her the score of a baseball game in which I was the home team and my opponent was the crisis of the moment. Sometimes the game was in the early innings, more often it was in the late innings because I prefer not to deal with things until they are immediate. Problems must wait their turn. If I mentioned a payment or note coming due or that we had money to last a certain number of days, she would respond in a predictable fashion by worrying and suggesting things for me to do, neither of which I welcomed. I simply wanted her to root for me or ask me in what way she could be of help. As with many families, money became a major silent subject for us.

I find the game of life exciting and challenging, not unlike an obstacle course. I derive great satisfaction in navigating through a tight spot. I like to "start out" and see what happens; to me that is adventure. I don't like guided tours, nor do I enjoy being a tourist. Marilou, on the other hand, didn't like surprises. She wanted to know what was next, and she liked to have money set aside for a rainy day. I don't mind walking in the rain.

"Worry on time."
G. NASH SMITH

Photo 37 – House under construction 1958

Photo 38 – Our home 1960

Photo 39 – Smith kids (from left: Cody, Tyle, Flint, Quade, Mocha) 1960

Photo 40 – The Outpost under construction 1960

Photo 41 – The Outpost roof 1961

Photo 42 – The Outpost 1962

Chapter 11

You Gotta Start Somewhere

Even though something generally went wrong on the climbs Marilou and I made together, some good did come from them. I knew what had to happen when the time was ripe to take each of the boys on their first 14er. The climb would have to be one of the easier mountains, and one that I had done so I knew what the boys were in for.

In September of 1962, when Flint was 10 years old and Quade was 6½, the three of us climbed Mount Sherman, their first 14er (see photo 43). All went well except for two things worth mentioning. The first was that Quade dislodged a large rock that landed on Flint's foot, causing a big "Oww." Lesson learned: watch where you step. The second was confirming the value of lemon drops, which I always carried. It turned out that Quade developed "cotton mouth," where his mouth and throat became extremely dry and he was having trouble breathing and swallowing. We solved it by having him suck on lemon drops.

Cody's first climb was Mount Democrat in August of 1964, two months after his 7th birthday (see photo 44). His two older and "more experienced" brothers went along, too. All went well.

Like Flint and Quade, 6-year-old Tyle's first 14er was Mount Sherman. He had been primed with a countdown approach. Five more months, four more months, five more weeks, four more weeks, five more days, four more days, three, two, one…. "Tomorrow we climb Mount Sherman, Tyle, are you ready?" "I think so," he said. Then presto, we were there.

Where was there? There was Fairplay, Colorado. We were all there, including Marilou and two dogs. If it hadn't been raining when we arrived we would have camped out. Instead, we rented only one room at Hotel Fairplay for the six of us because, as was the norm, we were short on funds. There was a single bed for Marilou and a rug-covered floor for the rest of us. The dogs were in the station wagon and would need to be let out at about 4 a.m.

The next morning, June 18, 1966, we drove towards the Leavick Mine. Five of us got ready to climb Mount Sherman. I would carry a pack, water, extra clothes, lemon drops, and some food. Flint was to lead the climb at first, and I would bring up the rear to take pictures.

Marilou stayed at the car with the two dogs. The route up this easy 14er followed a wagon road that in the late 1800s connected upper and lower mining operations. Before the climb got started, Tyle tripped and fell. He learned right away to watch where you step because the ground is not always flat. An auspicious debut for sure.

After hiking a distance about the length of a football field, Tyle began to whimper and stopped. He turned around and said, "Dad, I'm tired." It was at this time he got to hear the indoctrination speech each of his brothers before him had "enjoyed." I knelt down, put my arm around him and said, "We have barely started and you feel tired. I know the feeling quite well. But what you need to learn is that you don't stop when you are tired. You might slow down, but you don't stop. Tyle, I want you to lead, so take some deep breaths to stretch your lungs and start out with a pace you think you can keep." And off we went. We did stop a couple of times, however, and each of his brothers took a turn leading. When we looked back the buildings seemed a lot smaller and Tyle was pleased with his progress. We made it to the top and signed the register (see photo 45). On the way down, Tyle was beaming. He was a chatterbox all the way back to the car where we were greeted by Marilou and the dogs. Now each of the boys had climbed a 14er.

"Give up? Not yet. You go until you can't go any longer,
and then you take one more step."
G. NASH SMITH

Photo 43 – Mt. Sherman, first 14er (from left: Flint, Quade) September 2, 1962

54

Photo 44 – Mt. Democrat, Cody's first 14er (from left: Cody, Quade, Flint) August 8, 1964

Photo 45 – Mt. Sherman, Tyle's first 14er (from left: Cody, Flint, Quade, Tyle) June 18, 1966

Chapter 12

There are three 14ers in the Needle Range in the southwest corner of the state. The easiest way to access them is by train. The Durango & Silverton Narrow Gauge Railroad runs between those two towns and is a major tourist attraction (see photo 46). During the summer there is one special train each day that accommodates hikers/climbers as well as tourists. It has a car just for backpacks and makes a stop at "Needleton," eleven miles from Silverton, to allow backpackers access to Windom and Sunlight Peaks, and Mount Eolus.

When I could get away from town on an upcoming weekend, I would ask, "Who wants to go climbing?" Climbs for the kids were optional. Each boy could choose whether to go or not. Over the 1965 Labor Day weekend, 9-year-old Quade was the only one to say "Yes" to the offer of climbing the three Needle Range 14ers. He and I left for Durango on Thursday. Marilou, her brother Art, and the three other Smith kids would follow on Friday in a second car. The plan was for them to enjoy the Colorado southwest, including Mesa Verde, and meet us in Durango on Sunday after our climb.

On Friday morning in Durango our backpacks were loaded into the climbers' luggage car. We boarded the train for Silverton and got off at Needleton, elevation 8,200 feet (see photo 47). There was no civilization at Needleton except for a couple of cabins, but there is a footbridge that crosses the Animas River, marking the start of a trail to the three 14ers and the wilderness beyond. Seven miles up, at approximately 11,000 feet, is Chicago Basin, a popular camping area.

I had a World War II Army pack and Quade had a frameless Boy Scout pack. Both contained some clothes, food, and a sleeping bag, and between us we carried water and old-style camping equipment, such as a cook pot, metal cups, metal silverware, a hatchet, matches, lemon drops, and a canvas tarp. Along the trail we saw lush meadow clearings and numerous places where water cascaded down from the sides of the valley, one of which is called "New York Creek." It seemed we had the whole valley to ourselves. We didn't see another person on the hike in.

To give ourselves the best chance to climb the three mountains tomorrow, we chose to camp at the far end of Chicago Basin before the trail got steep (see photo 48). There was a nice area for our sleeping bags and plenty of wood. During dinner we discussed our time deadline and what had to happen for us to catch the train on Sunday. The hiker/climber train passes through Needleton at 11:15 a.m. on the way to Silverton, and 2:10 p.m. on the way back from Silverton, and will only stop if someone flags it. If you're not at Needleton in time to catch the 2:10 p.m. train, you are out of luck until the next day. Starting from Chicago Basin a strong team can climb all three 14ers in one day. That was our goal, too, but our capabilities were unknown. We would just give it our best.

On Saturday morning, it was overcast. We had a light breakfast and I packed my pack. We headed up a steep trail into the high basin between the three peaks that form an elongated triangle, with Windom and Sunlight Peaks relatively close to each other to the east and Mount Eolus a mile and a half to their west. We worked our way to the ridge of Windom and followed it to the top. It had rained off and on all morning. When we signed the register, the valley was filling with swirling clouds that resembled steam rising from a mammoth boiling vat of a witch's brew. We headed in the direction of Sunlight Peak, which was hidden in the clouds. By the time we reached its base the clouds had lifted. The top of Sunlight is unique and rugged, so the register is kept below the true summit (see photo 49). Hooray! Success! Two mountains down and one to go.

To climb Mount Eolus the suggested route was up its south face from Chicago Basin, which meant we could start from where our camp was. It was 3 p.m. when we got there, according to Quade's Timex wristwatch. I thought we would need five hours round trip to climb Mount Eolus in good conditions, but because it was raining it would take us longer and we would run out of daylight.

Our goal was still to catch the train tomorrow at 2:10 p.m. So, we had a decision to make. Do we start early in the morning from here or do we whittle away at the 3,000 feet this afternoon? We chose to whittle away. We left Quade's stuff at camp. I took my sleeping bag, which was big enough for both of us, a tarp, cheese and crackers, and some water, and we headed up. "Maybe the rain won't last long," I said to Quade. And it didn't. It turned to snow. But we kept going. By 4:30 p.m. there was an inch of the white stuff on the ground. The snowflakes were extra-large and it was beautiful watching them shake hands with the earth. At about 4:45 p.m. we came across a ledge at the base of a rock wall that was wide enough to hold our sleeping bag so we chose to stop there for the day.

The ground wasn't quite flat but I was able to level it with a tool I had found earlier. It was a sixteen-inch-long, three-quarter-inch-diameter rod that had a chisel-like nose, that no doubt was left over from mining days. We both crawled into the one sleeping bag at 5 p.m. For dinner we had Ritz crackers and Kraft pimento cheese spread. We were done for the day. There was nothing else to do but try and get some sleep.

The next morning, our Cony's eye view from the snow-covered grassy rim was one of the prettiest ever, what with at least four inches of fresh snow and a crisp, slowly-getting-lighter sky with just a few clouds. If we had wanted to toboggan all the way down to Chicago Basin, we could've done so by moving our sleeping bag sideways a couple of feet. It would've been a nice morning to stay in bed, except that is where we had been for fourteen hours.

At 7 a.m. we left our wet bivouac gear and headed up. We still had a mountain to climb and a train to catch. The snow was melting, which made the rock wet and slippery and slowed us down. It was 10 a.m. when we signed the Mount Eolus register. We only had four hours to catch the train. It didn't look good.

After an hour of heading down, Chicago Basin came into view. We sat down to rest and decide what to do. We would split up. Quade would go to camp, pick up his backpack and sleeping bag and hustle down the trail on his own. I would go get last night's tarp and sleeping bag, then pick up the rest of our stuff at camp, and chase after Quade. I had Quade point out where he thought camp was and the route he would take to get there. I told him if he couldn't find the trail and then our camp, he was to sit down, holler periodically and listen for my response. It is not a good idea for two people to be hunting for each other. Only one should hunt while the other stays put.

Because the grassy slope was wet and slick it took me longer than I thought it would to get to the tarp and sleeping bag. When I got back to camp, Quade's pack was gone, which was a good sign. I gathered up everything, and headed down the trail. It was several miles before I caught Quade, and when I did, he asked for water and said his feet hurt. I replied, "We don't have any water, but maybe we can get some at New York Creek. Re-tie your boots extra tight, that should help your feet. We need to move fast. You lead."

We got to New York Creek at 1:50 p.m. That gave us only twenty minutes to go two miles, so we didn't stop for water. Even though we had been close to running the whole time I said to Quade, "We've gotta go faster. Keep your rhythm but stretch your stride. Even a couple of inches will help. Hang in there, kid; you can do it." We continued moving like two packhorses, and we were sweating like three packhorses. Hup, two, three, four, double-time. My toes hit the front of my $8.50 J. C. Penney work boots with each step. My feet were killing me. Our packs slapped us on the back in a rhythm I can still feel and hear. It wasn't raining, but we were soaked.

Hup, two, three, four, double-time. We heard a train whistle echo in the valley. I wasn't sure what that meant but I was afraid it wasn't good. We crossed the foot bridge at Needleton. Splat! Down we went to the ground without bothering to remove our packs. It was 2:20 p.m. Here's hoping the train was late. Our bodies were hurting in all kinds of ways. After a few more minutes we were pretty sure we had missed the train. "Darn it."

We took our packs off and removed our boots. Our socks were stuck to the knuckles of our toes with blood. Then we limped a short distance down to the Animas River and soaked our feet. While we were sitting there in the soothing water, we could faintly hear what sounded like the pounding of a hammer. We put our boots back on, carried our stuff back across the bridge, set it down, and then went to learn what the sound was.

There were two guys working on an A-frame that was snuggled nicely in the tall trees. It turned out a handyman was helping a couple who owned the property. The men had seen us running down the trail, and we were told the train had passed through about ten minutes ahead of us. Ten minutes. What a great effort to be only ten lousy minutes late.

That night, we shared a tasty dinner with the couple. It was the first real meal we had had in three days. They also offered us their bunkhouse for the night, which we gratefully accepted. We slept like cement slabs. The windows were open to the crisp, night air and Quade remembers being weighed down with layers of heavy blankets. The bed felt really good. In the morning, after a breakfast that was as good as dinner had been, Quade drank coffee for the first time. We offered to help with chores in an effort to repay the couple for their hospitality but they didn't have anything for us to do.

Quade and I caught the 11:15 a.m. train going to Silverton and became tourists (see photo 50). We enjoyed lunch, then took the train back to Durango, and guess who was waiting for us? A worried group of family members.

Before we told them what really happened, I said, "We decided to take an extra day because it was so beautiful." Then I told them how proud I was of Quade for the job he had done. I knew from that experience I wouldn't have to worry about Quade. That nine-year-old boy would make it. Now there were just three more boys to teach. I was "practically there."

"Do your best to do your best."
G. NASH SMITH

Photo 46 – Durango & Silverton Narrow Gauge Railroad September 2, 1965

Photo 47 – Needleton bridge Labor Day weekend

Photo 48 – Chicago Basin, Sunlight Peak is in the center and Windom Peak is to the right

Photo 49 – Quade below the summit of Sunlight Peak, 30 feet below the register (oriented as taken, blurred photo) September 3, 1965

Photo 50 – Quade riding Narrow-Gauge Train after climbing Needle Mountains September 5, 1965

Chapter 13

A FIVE-DOLLAR BRIBE

Quade had proved his worthiness on our climb of Windom, Sunlight and Eolus in September of 1965. The other three boys became indoctrinated together on August 20, 1966, on Mount Columbia. If Mocha, our dog, could talk she would probably agree that that was a really tough day. *Following are Tyle's recollections of the climb with input from everyone.*

Mount Columbia was my 8th 14er and we climbed it just after I had turned seven. We drove from Denver that morning, planning to approach Columbia from the east. We followed a jeep road partway up Frenchman Creek, where we left the car and started hiking.

When we began the weather was partly cloudy and pleasant. We left the road and bushwhacked to a ridge that we thought would take us to the top. It soon started to drizzle and then turned to rain. It wasn't a heavy rain but it was relentless, chilly, and very frustrating. It rained off and on all day (see photos 51, 52).

A couple hours into the climb, my hands were quite cold and wet. My mittens were soaked and I was whimpering (see photo 53). We were all soaked, especially Mocha. Dad came to my rescue and warmed my hands. He wasn't wearing gloves and he seemed fine. Wow, I remember thinking how impressed I was with Dad. He was an amazingly tough man.

We kept running into false peak after false peak and it was getting late, but Dad wanted us to make it to the top. At about 6 p.m., after reaching yet another false peak, us kids finally got up enough gumption to say, "C'mon Dad, this is no fun. Let's go back." Dad countered, "I'll tell you what. If this next peak isn't the summit, then I'll give each of you five dollars." Somehow that appeased us, and I lit up because my monthly allowance was only fifty cents. We decided to go on and claim our money, but sure enough, that was the top of Columbia. So, not only were we wet and cold but we didn't get our five dollars (see photo 54).

Finally, we were headed down and the rain had stopped. I was feeling better about our situation. It was getting dark, and by the time we got below timberline it was darker yet. There was no moonlight. We found the road but the trees made a canopy over us that blocked what starlight might have shone from the night sky.

Because we were on the road and not on open terrain, Dad pulled out the flashlight. He always carried a flashlight but prefers not to use it until it's necessary. Once the light of a flashlight is introduced, a hiker becomes dependent on that light source. If a flashlight fails, it takes a while for one's eyes to adjust again to the darkness. Dad was in front, swinging the flashlight back and forth to illuminate the road and help us avoid rocks. We followed him using the periodic light as best we could.

Dad had a system of counting to keep track of us in this type of situation. Regardless of our hiking order, us kids would count off numerically, Flint was 1, Quade was 2, Cody was 3, and I was 4.

It had been a really long day and we were exhausted, so after walking for a while we took a break and sat down on the road; and Dad turned off the flashlight. We could not see each other because our eyes were still used to its light.

The next thing I remember is hearing someone say, "Hey, Tyle, get up," and I woke up to the light of a flashlight in my face. It turns out, I had fallen asleep, and so had Mocha. They had all started down the road towards the car without me and after a short distance, Dad said, "Count off." He heard in reply, "1, 2, 3," but there was no "4." Number 4 was asleep on the road! They had to come back to get me and Mocha.

It was after midnight when we finally got to the car. We had hiked eighteen miles in fourteen hours. This climb was quite a life lesson. I learned that a day's effort might carry over into the next day, but if I kept moving and didn't quit, I would eventually get there. I just had to put my mind to it and keep going.

"Keep going. Some of the best memories come from adverse conditions."
G. Nash Smith

Photo 51 – Rain break on climb of Mount Columbia (from left: Flint, Quade, Mocha, Tyle, Cody)

August 20, 1966

Photo 52 – Skies cleared for a moment (from left: Cody, Mocha, Quade, Flint, Tyle)

Photo 53 – Tyle showing frustration for being cold and wet and still having a long way to go

Photo 54 – Top of Columbia (from left: Quade, Tyle, Cody, Mocha, Flint) August 20, 1966

Chapter 14

CREEK CROSSING

Our climbs in 1966 and 1967 helped us increase our general mountain-eering knowledge and skills. We had been successful on some moderately challenging 14ers already without the use of any technical climbing equip-ment, including ropes and belaying techniques. By the end of July 1967 we felt we were ready to tackle some of the tougher 14ers, one of which is Pyramid Peak. The four Smith kids, Marilou and I drove to Aspen on Saturday, July 29, 1967, and set up camp near Maroon Lake, planning to climb Pyramid the next day (see photo 55).

On Sunday morning, we broke camp, drove to the trailhead and got ready for the climb. We said "goodbye" to Mom, who had a book to read. We hiked about a half hour on the trail towards Crater Lake, with West Maroon Creek to our left. We then crossed where the creek was underground and headed up over a ridge which put us on the right side of a large basin called the Amphitheater (see photo 56). Keeping a high traverse to maintain our elevation, we headed to the shoulder on the right side of Pyramid. We turned left, and gained more elevation until we reached a mass of broken, rocky ledges and a series of couloirs about 1,000 feet below the summit. A couloir is a steep, "v"-shaped gulley or chute that adds danger because it funnels any dislodged rocks downward and is hazardous to climbers below. Pyramid Peak has more than its share of these rocky couloirs.

In an attempt to minimize the chance of dislodging a rock, we had two strategies. One being to send one boy at a time up a couloir until he reached a safe ledge and got out of the way. When he was no longer at risk of dislodging any rocks he would holler, "clear," and the next boy would go. If anyone did happen to knock a rock loose, he would immediately holler, "rock," to warn everyone below to look up, watch for the rock and react accordingly. The other strategy was to ascend a couloir in group for-mation, following each other closely so that if a rock was dislodged the next climber in line could stop it before it went anywhere. We took pride in safely navigating rocky couloirs.

On many climbs, man-made stacks of rocks called "cairns" have been placed by someone, suggesting a route to follow going up or down. On Pyramid Peak, following cairns was not a good idea because there were too many to choose from. So, Flint was sent ahead to scout the best route for us. We would ascend a couloir or two, then traverse, then ascend again. Sometimes we stayed on a ledge and traversed past one couloir to take the next and then ascend that one. The route was complex with no set pattern, but 15-year-old Flint did a good job of route finding.

I re-emphasized to the boys the importance of frequently looking back to help memorize the terrain for a successful return (see photos 57, 58).

We topped out, signed the register at around 4 p.m., took a few pictures, and headed down (see photos 59-61). Because it was getting dark, we decided not to retrace our steps from this morning. We intended to save time and distance by trying to reach the trail closer to Maroon Lake. So, instead of traversing high, we dropped down into the amphitheater and exited through its mouth (see photo 62). Then we turned right, heading more directly towards Maroon Lake. It turned out that wasn't a good idea because we encountered a series of cliffs that continually pushed us to the left, away from our target. We used a small-diameter, fifty-foot rope to descend the cliffs.

When we finally reached the valley floor it was pitch dark, and there were willows to deal with plus a creek to cross. The creek was aboveground, unlike our morning crossing, and was running high, because of the day's snowmelt. To cross the creek we formed a human chain, facing upstream, joining forearms and moving sideways. Flint was leading, then Cody, then Quade, then Tyle, and then me. The water was up to Tyle's chest and we dared not let go of him. Luckily, the creek bottom was not rocky, making it easier for solid foot placements. Once on the other side, we found the trail and headed for the car. On the way we met Marilou, who had started up the trail with a flashlight to look for us. She was quite relieved to see us and we were really glad to see her. The climb had taken us fourteen hours round-trip. We had a four-hour drive, getting home at 3 in the morning. Talk about a long day, good job!

"Poor judgment in route finding can be hazardous to your health."
G. NASH SMITH

Photo 55 – Pyramid camp (from left: Marilou, Flint, Cody, Quade) July 1967

Photo 56 – Approaching traverse above the Pyramid amphitheater July 30, 1967

Photo 57 – Cody and Quade looking back to remember the route

Photo 58 – Look closely for Cody and Quade ascending slopes of Pyramid with North Maroon to the left and Snowmass in the distance

Photo 59 – Top of Pyramid (from left: Flint, Cody, Tyle, Quade) note the construction boots July 30, 1967

Photo 60 – Tyle and Cody atop Pyramid with Snowmass Mountain (back left) and Capitol Peak (back center)

Photo 61 – Going down Pyramid Peak couloir (from left: Cody, Quade)

Photo 62 – Amphitheater descent

Chapter 15

Let's Climb 'em All

At the beginning of the 1967 climbing season, the kids all seemed to enjoy the mountains. However, the idea to climb all of the Colorado 14ers as a family had not yet been born, except within me. The youngest person of record to have climbed all of the 14ers in Colorado was Bob Melzer, a 9-year-old boy, who climbed them with his dad, Carl, in 1937. When I was with Monte Carroll & Co. in the late 1950s, Grace Melzer, Bob's mother, was also there as a salesperson and we talked 14ers many times.

And what do you know, at dinner on Sunday, June 4, the day after we Smiths had climbed Pikes Peak, Flint brought up the idea of climbing all of the 14ers as a family. After talking about it we took a vote. It was unanimous! We would do it! So, that became our family goal, and we would try to get it done before Tyle turned 9 on July 24 next year. At this time he had made it to the top of thirteen 14ers and only needed forty more. We were practically there!

In those days, when a climber signed a summit register, most would sign as being affiliated with a group of some kind, such as the Colorado Mountain Club, Boulder Mountain Club, El Paso Mountain Club, etc. And for me, not to be outdone, I had been signing as "OMC" which had been short for "Own Mountain Club." Now, because of our new family goal, I wanted "OMC" to represent something more and changed the name to "Outpost Mountain Club," in honor of our dance hall.

In 1967 I was calling square dances for the "Promenaders," a singles group that met weekly at the Denver YMCA. My fee was $10.00. One of the dancers was Virginia Nolan, a member of the Colorado Mountain Club. She was the fortieth person to have climbed all of Colorado's recognized 14ers, having finished with a climb of Crestone Peak in 1952. The Crestones (Needle and Peak), are two of the four 14ers in the Sangre de Cristo range near the town of Westcliffe, and were next on our list to do. So far this summer we had climbed twelve new 14ers, and because the Crestones were considered to be tough climbs I thought we could use some help. Earlier, I had asked Virginia if she would lead us and she declined, but said she would check with her friend, Bill Arnold, to see if he would be interested. He lived in Pueblo and was a member of the El Paso Mountain Club, and was the thirty-third person to have climbed them all. Bill said "Yes" to leading us. And because of that, Virginia said she would join us. The hike was planned for early August.

The last seven miles of the South Colony Lakes road, which is the suggested approach to climb the four peaks, requires a 4WD vehicle so I had rented a Jeep Wagoneer. We met Bill and Virginia where they had parked at the start of the 4WD section on Friday morning, August 4. They had carpooled and were in a sedan. The Wagoneer wasn't big enough for seven people plus gear. So, I needed to perform two shuttles. The four Smith kids were in the first load, but before we reached the end of the road, as luck would have it, we got a flat. We changed tires and then drove to the trailhead where I dropped the kids off with their gear. They packed in the one mile to lower South Colony Lake to set up camp while I went back to do the second shuttle (see photos 63-65). That afternoon, Bill and Virginia set up their camp and we Smiths climbed Humboldt Peak, which was a four-hour round trip (see photos 66-69). The plan was for all of us to climb the Crestones tomorrow, and we Smiths would then climb Kit Carson on Sunday to complete the four peaks.

At 6:30 on Saturday morning the seven of us started up Crestone Needle. The rock was conglomerate and offered many big, solid handholds (see photos 70, 71). The climb went well. We got to the summit in three and a half hours (see photo 72). Now to Crestone Peak. Virginia pointed out a route off the top that she had once taken which avoided an immediate and exposed forty-foot rappel down a nearly vertical face. Bill would lead. There were numerous ridges, gulleys and pinnacles to cross (see photos 73-75). Clouds surrounded us and it began to rain lightly. We came to a tough section and used ropes for the first time. Virginia belayed us across a traverse to Bill and then he belayed us down a steep wall.

To quote Bill Arnold:
"Although the ropes got tangled a little, the whole party negotiated the delicate pitch without a slip" (see photo 76). I had to admire the Smiths for this performance... During the day I had been quite favorably impressed by the Smith boys' climbing ability, especially that of Flint, the oldest, and of Tyle, the youngest. The way George got around was something to behold, too."

We got on top of Crestone Peak after a six-hour traverse (see photo 77). From the Peak back to camp was another three and a half, for a round-trip total of thirteen hours.

To quote Virginia Nolan:

"It was at timberline on a soft summer evening that I met the Smith boys... I had had some qualms about climbing the Crestones, two of Colorado's more difficult peaks, with this young a group. I had always climbed with a more mature group and for some queer reason, felt that it took age to produce a good climber. I could not have been further wrong.

"What impressed me the most throughout the entire climb was their team work. I could never quite figure out whether each of the older boys was assigned to a particular younger boy, or whether it was their policy to always have one of the older boys climbing with one of the younger boys. In any case, they tackled the mountain like veterans. Their father brought up the rear which made for an ideal team pattern. The entire team could adapt to any change without so much as a halt and without (with) very little or no comment.

"My hard hat is off to the Climbing Smiths."

The next day, we Smiths climbed Kit Carson Peak, which is also considered to be one of the tougher Colorado 14ers. We had a rope with us but didn't use it (see photos 78-81). A group of climbers from the El Paso Section of the Colorado Mountain Club showed interest in our route selection and followed us. We topped out, signed the register (see photo 82), and headed back to camp. It hailed pretty good on the way but we were done with the tough parts by then. The climb had taken us about twelve hours. We broke camp, hiked to the Jeep, drove down the 4WD road and back to Denver. Our thanks go to Bill and Virginia for helping us climb the Crestones.

Photo 63 – Pack in to South Colony Lakes (from left: Flint, Cody, Tyle, Quade) August 4, 1967

Photo 64 – Cody looking at Crestone Needle

Photo 65 – South Colony Lakes camp (from left: Flint, Quade, Cody)

Photo 66 – Starting up Humboldt Peak

Photo 67 – The Crestones: Needle (left), Peak (right), as viewed from Humboldt

Photo 68 – Fog setting in on summit approach

Photo 69 – Top of Humboldt (from left: Quade, Flint, Cody, Tyle) August 4, 1967

Photo 70 – On the way up Crestone Needle August 5, 1967

Photo 71 – Working the rock on Crestone Needle

Photo 72 – Crestone Needle summit (from left: Virginia Nolan, Bill Arnold, Cody, Tyle, Flint, Quade)
Crestone Peak on the right August 5, 1967

Photo 73 – Traversing between Crestone Needle and Peak

Photo 74 – Downclimbing

Photo 75 – Traversing the ridge to Crestone Peak

Photo 76 – Two roped teams at work between the Crestones

Photo 77 – Crestone Peak (from left: Quade, Tyle, Virginia, Bill, Cody, Flint) August 5, 1967

Photo 78 – On the way to Kit Carson August 6, 1967

Photo 79 – Smith kids on Kit Carson Peak (from left: Flint, Quade, Tyle, Cody)

Photo 80 – View to Kit Carson hidden behind false peak

Photo 81 - Climbing Kit Carson's false peak

Photo 82 - Kit Carson summit (from left: Flint, Quade, Cody, Tyle) August 6, 1967

Chapter 16

Postholing

The shortest route to climb Blanca and Little Bear Peaks, which are in southern Colorado near the town of Alamosa, starts near Como Lake. But the road to Como Lake requires the use of a 4WD vehicle, which we didn't have. So, along with Mocha, our dog, we chose to climb them from the south in a two-day effort. On Saturday, June 22, 1968, the day after we had climbed Mount Lindsey, we woke (see photo 83) and drove north from the town of Blanca on a dirt road through Arrowhead Lodge, which is private property, and required permission. When the road stopped we began backpacking on a game trail, planning to hike several miles and then find a place to spend the night. But the game trail soon quit. So we backtracked and took another game trail (see photos 84, 85) and worked our way through brush for four and a half miles before we came to an unoccupied cabin. We decided to spend the night there on the flat ground next to it. We put down the tarp and sleeping bags and Mocha curled up among us. It was 8 p.m.

In the morning, we left our backpacks, I took my daypack, and we headed for Little Bear. We crossed over a bunch of irregular rocks of various sizes and shapes and quite a few of them had rough edges. Due to the steepness of the slope we had to scramble at times, using our hands for added balance and support. We had a goldline rope with us but we didn't need to use it (see photos 86, 87).

After four hours, we reached the summit of Little Bear (see photo 88), and then headed for Blanca Peak. The ridge to Blanca looked rugged and would be extra slow-going because Mocha was with us (see photo 89). So, we dropped down on the south side below the ridge and traversed across snow, which filled the basin. The snow was crusty on top and we got a good dose of "postholing." Postholing is when your foot breaks through crusty snow and requires extra effort to lift your leg and take the next step. Plus, you run the risk of ankle or ligament damage. The traverse from Little Bear to Blanca took three hours to cover a fat mile due to the postholing, and really zapped us.

It was 5 p.m. when we finally signed in on Blanca (see photo 90). After a half-hour break, which is longer than usual, we began our return. We got back to the cabin, gathered everything and started walking the four and a half miles to the car. We were moving slower than normal because everybody, including Mocha, walked with a limp of some kind. It was 10:30 p.m. when we reached our car.

Because of this climb we have a bit of family humor that we still use today. When a family member or close friend shows up walking with a limp, it might be suggested that he or she looks like they just got off of Blanca. At my age, every time I walk I look like I just got off of Blanca.

Photo 83 – Breaking camp prior to heading for Little Bear and Blanca Peaks June 22, 1968

Photo 84 – Not camping here, just resting on the way (from left: Mocha, Cody, Tyle, Flint, Quade)
note large, heavy sleeping bags

Photo 85 – Backpack approach to Little Bear Peak

Photo 86 – Working the ridge to Little Bear June 23, 1968

Photo 87 – Below the summit of Little Bear (from left: George, Tyle, Flint, Mocha, Cody, Quade)

Photo 88 – Top of Little Bear (from left: Mocha, Cody, Flint, Tyle, Quade) June 23, 1968

Photo 89 – View of the ridge to Blanca from Little Bear

Photo 90 – Summit of Blanca Peak (from left: Flint, George, Mocha, Cody, Quade) June 23, 1968

Chapter 17

Hang on, Tyle!

Following are Flint's recollections about climbing Capitol Peak with input from all of us. It has been more than fifty years since we climbed Capitol Peak the first time. It was our forty-sixth Colorado 14er. Back then there were two main references for route finding, Robert Ormes' *Guide to the Colorado Mountains*, and the Colorado Mountain Club's *Condensed Climber's Guide to Colorado's Highest Peaks*, both of which we had had problems following, so we typically ended up doing our own route selection. Dad gave me that responsibility. We relied on visual landmarks, sometimes USGS topographical maps, and occasionally a compass.

Capitol was a climb that we thought would need a pack in. Included in our backpacks would be sleeping gear, water, clothes, and some food. Dad had the tarp and lemon drops and we had group gear to divvy up, a rope, and cooking equipment.

On Friday, June 28, 1968, we arrived at the Capitol Creek Trailhead about 5:30 p.m. and started hiking around 6 p.m. We dropped down 500 vertical feet into the Capitol Creek basin. The basin was filled with crisscrossing cattle trails, none of which seemed to be going where we wanted to go. We worked our way up the valley and found the main trail, but it was getting dark. We ended up camping below timberline a couple of miles short of where we had planned to get.

The next morning, we began our ascent. Only Dad had a pack and I had a rope. We followed the trail several miles, then turned off just before Capitol Lake (see photos 91, 92), aiming for the low point of the ridge, called the saddle. From there I led us up the ridge until we reached a rugged part called the "cockscomb." To work the cockscomb was visibly the shortest route, but it was really time-consuming because it went up and down, and up and down, like the cockscomb of a rooster (see photo 93). We were pretty good at scrambling but it took way too long to get across this ridge which required extensive use of hands. When we finished the cockscomb section we still had more ridge to follow to get to a subpeak called "K2."

From K2 we took in the view south to three 14ers we still needed to do (see photo 94), and then dropped down sixty feet to the famous "knife edge." The knife edge of Capitol is granite rock known for its exposure. It consists of three sections of a horizontal ridge at 13,600 feet in elevation with a steep drop-off of several hundred feet on either side. Because of the exposure and sharp angle, these sections look dramatically like the blade of a knife, hence the name, "knife edge."

Many groups use a rope to belay one another across the knife edge. We didn't. Instead, we chose to scoot across (see photo 95). We have trust in each other and our abilities and we do not use a rope unless someone asks for one. Once across the knife edge we still had five hundred feet of elevation to gain to reach the summit. We arrived there just before 6 p.m., took a photo and headed back towards the knife edge and K2 (see photos 96, 97). This time we felt more confident and walked across the knife edge (see photo 98).

It was late so we needed to decide what was next. We knew using the cockscomb to return would be slow going. So, our plan was to descend the east side of the cockscomb ridge, traverse across the talus slope, made up of medium-to-large-sized rocks, and work our way towards the saddle.

During the traverse we encountered sections of steep snow, which hardened as night fell and the temperature dropped. I led by vigorously punching my heels downward into the snow to go downhill and kicking with the toe of my boots to traverse sideways, trying to make footsteps that everyone could safely use. During the traverse we had lost some elevation which we would need to regain to get to the saddle.

I came to a section of snow that was very steep and exposed and was just above a rock face. It was almost dark now and I told Dad we should cross this section one at a time and use a rope. He agreed. So I took one end of our goldline rope while he held the other end. I kicked steps across the snow until I was on solid terrain and set myself up as an anchor. The plan was for each of my brothers to cross over and up to me, using the rope as a kind of bannister for stability. They would face inwards, moving sideways, using the steps I had made. Tyle was first.

Tyle, at age 7, had learned to climb with care and sound technique but while traversing he somehow slipped. I felt a sudden jolt on the rope and knew something had happened. It turns out Tyle was hanging onto the rope with both hands extended overhead with his belly touching the rock wall. He was struggling to find a foothold and yelled for help. All I could do was keep anchoring my end of the rope and wait as Dad quickly sent Quade to help Tyle regain his footing. When Tyle got to me I was relieved. Quade followed, then Cody and then Dad. We thanked the Lord above and knew we had dodged a bullet. We thought that was a really close call, but Tyle assured us that he wasn't going to let go.

Because it was quite dark and route finding was a problem, we knew we had to hunker down for the night. After gaining a little more elevation we found a flat, protected area just below the ridge where we could group together for warmth. We never planned on spending the night high on a mountain but that night we would. Nobody got much sleep. Quade's feet were cold so he loosened his boots for better circulation. We periodically would stand and stomp our feet to try to keep warm.

Morning could not come soon enough and because we were on the east side of the ridge, the sun hit us early, providing some warmth, and that felt good. We spent the night higher than the saddle so we had to descend to it. We made our way to camp, ate a snack, gathered our stuff and then headed out (see photo 99). The car was a welcome sight! Wow! That was a climb and a half!

"I can still do a day's work but it might be sometime tomorrow before I am finished."
G. NASH SMITH

Photo 91 – View of Capitol Peak June 29, 1968

Photo 92 – Approaching Capitol Lake

Photo 93 – On the cockscomb ridge going towards Capitol

Photo 94 – View from K2 of Pierre Basin, Maroon Bells (far left) and Snowmass

Photo 95 – Crossing the knife edge

Photo 96 – Capitol Peak summit (from left: Flint, Tyle, Quade, Cody) June 29, 1968

Photo 97 – Heading back

Photo 98 – Re-crossing the knife edge

Photo 99 – Packing out the morning after bivouacking on the ridge

Chapter 18

Native American Chant

Following are Quade's recollections of the climb of El Diente Peak with input from all of us.

Before I talk about our successful climb of El Diente in 1968, I want to tell you about our failed attempt the summer before. We planned a long trip to the San Juans over the July 4th holiday in 1967. On Sunday, July 2nd, after we had climbed Mount Sneffels, we drove up the road to the Silver Pick Mine and camped, preparing to climb the two Wilsons and El Diente the next day. On Monday morning we started hiking up the road at 8:15 a.m. and headed towards the 13,000-foot ridge above the Rock of Ages Mine. Once on the ridge we turned left to climb Wilson Peak, the easiest of the Wilsons. We were successful. On our descent we passed by the Rock of Ages Mine at about 2:30 p.m. Since the weather was good we headed to Mount Wilson, hoping to climb El Diente as well. We did succeed in reaching the summit of the tougher Wilson but we thought it was too late to tackle the mile-long ridge to El Diente. It turns out that was a good choice because we didn't get back to the Rock of Ages Mine until 10 p.m. Because we still wanted to climb El Diente we decided to bivouac there instead of hiking back to the car where our sleeping bags were. We put on all the extra clothes Dad had in his pack because at nearly 13,000 feet we knew it was gonna get cold.

The next morning, we headed for El Diente but after a few hours we turned around. We were beat because of a lousy night's sleep, plus we got a late start. And besides that, we took a bad route up the north face and spent time hung up on a rib of rock. We could have bailed out onto the hard snow but didn't feel comfortable with its steepness. So, we called it quits for the day and returned to the car. We went on to climb all five of the San Juan Peaks near Lake City in the next four days before heading home. It was frustrating to not get to the top; but the good news was El Diente would not be going anywhere.

In 1968 on July 4, 5, and 6 we did the Durango train ride again because Flint, Cody and Tyle needed to climb Windom, Sunlight and Eolus. On July 6th we packed out of Chicago Basin, caught the afternoon train at Needleton and got back to Durango in the late afternoon. (That round-trip train ride for the five of us cost a total of $20.60).

Now, finally, I can tell you about our successful climb of El Diente. After we got a bite to eat in Durango we drove 100-plus miles to the Silver Pick Mine road. Part way up the seven-mile dirt road to the mine there was too much snow so we pulled off and camped. Even though it was July, the road had patches of snow on it, well below 11,000 feet, which made it impassable for our vehicle. So, at 11:30 p.m. we laid out our tarp and sleeping bags for the night.

The next morning, July 7, we started hiking at 8 a.m. It took us two and a half hours on the snow-covered road to get to the Rock of Ages Mine. This was longer than we expected because we had to do a lot of postholing. The clouds were thick and low and it was snowing. That figures, we get a lot of that. The weather wasn't good and the visibility was poor, but we decided to keep going anyway (see photo 100).

After dropping down 800 feet into Navajo Basin, we started up the north face of El Diente, but the storm got worse (see photos 101, 102). Now what? We didn't want El Diente to beat us a second time. We found a flat rock that was big enough for all of us to stand on and wait out the storm. At 2 p.m. we huddled under a tarp and began to stomp our feet in rhythm (See photo 103). We started to chant. Chant? What chant?

It turns out on an earlier family vacation to Carlsbad Caverns, on a restaurant wall in New Mexico, we had seen what Dad thought was probably a Native American poem or chant. He wrote down the words, and while we don't know its actual meaning, we adopted it for our own use to combat bad weather and we really needed it today.

"WE-YA HEY-YA NA-YA
HA-YO HA-YO HI-YA
WE-YO HAI-YO HAI-YO
YO-HA YA-NA HI-YA YA-NA."
Author Unknown

It took an hour for the chant to work but it did work and the weather started to clear. We then made our way up a snowy couloir to the ridge and followed it to the summit, signing the register at 6 p.m. The ascent had taken us seven hours from the Rock of Ages Mine, including the hour of successful chanting (see photos 104-107). After about fifteen minutes we headed down (see photos 108, 109), getting back to the Rock of Ages Mine at 8:45 p.m. and our car at

10:30 p.m. We then headed back through Gunnison, driving all night, getting home at 6:30 in the morning. We were relieved to have finally done El Diente.

"You don't learn what is important to learn if you only show up when it's sunny."
G. NASH SMITH

Photo 100 – Looking towards El Diente Peak from Rock of Ages Mine July 7, 1968

Photo 101 – Dropping down into Navajo Basin in a snowstorm on the way to El Diente

Photo 102 – Working our way up El Diente

Photo 103 – Chanting to stop the storm

Photo 104 – El Diente couloir

Photo 105 – El Diente Ridge connecting to Mount Wilson

Photo 106 – Working the ridge and sharing a pair of mittins

Photo 107 – On top of El Diente (from left: Cody, Quade, Tyle, Flint) July 7, 1968

Photo 108 – Going down

Photo 109 – Sliding on snow towards Navajo Basin

Chapter 19

Thanks, Bill Arnold

After climbing El Diente last week on July 7, 1968, we only had the Maroon Bells and Snowmass Mountain left to do. In 1954 Warren and I had climbed North Maroon by itself, and that was a major challenge. The boys and I wanted to climb both North Maroon Peak and Maroon Peak together and knew we had to cross the tough ridge between them to do that. That summer, to get ready for the Bells ridge we practiced rappelling at home off one of the buildings on our property. We placed a two-inch by twelve-inch plank on a ladder against a shed. We anchored our goldline rope and, while facing "uphill," leaned back and rappelled down the plank (see photo 110). We practiced a Dülfersitz rappel, which involves wrapping the rope around one's body in an "S" curve to create friction and control one's rate of descent. When using a Dülfersitz rappel, no special technical equipment other than a rope is needed, which fit our budget. We thought this skill might be useful when crossing the ridge.

In June I had asked Virginia Nolan to lead us on our climb of the Bells, which I had scheduled for July 13, but she was not able to do it. Virginia talked to Bill Arnold and he said that date would work for him. He and his wife, Kay, planned to meet us at a campground near Maroon Lake on the evening of July 12, 1968, which they did.

At 6:20 the next morning, we all left the parking lot, including Kay, who went as far as Crater Lake (see photo 111). With Bill Arnold leading, we got to the top of North Maroon Peak at 1:15 p.m. without any problems. After a half-hour lunch break, we started across the ridge to Maroon Peak. The ridge is technical and slow going. While the distance between the peaks is just over a quarter mile as the crow flies, it took us a little over two and a half hours to cross it. On one section Bill provided a top rope, belaying everyone down a short wall, except Flint, who rappelled; and then Bill rappelled. (see photos 112-116).

We made our way to Maroon Peak and signed the summit register at 4:15 p.m. After fifteen minutes we headed down the south ridge towards the shoulder and the snow couloir. When we got there, because the snow conditions seemed good, we decided to descend the couloir and not follow the ridge any further (see photos 117-121). We tied two ropes together to make one long length for six people, and used what is known as a "plunge-step" to descend to the valley floor with the rope being used for safety. Plunge-stepping is an action of descending snow by vigorously plunging one's heels down into the snow to make steps using straight-legged, toe-raised, heel thrusts. Bill had an ice axe so he was the last person in our roped team. If needed, he could use his ice axe to perform a self-arrest and stop our fall if someone slipped (see photo 122).

Bill was a capable climber and we were confident in our safety. We realized, however, that we had work to do to become proficient in the use of an ice axe on steep snow and in icy conditions. We reached the trail leading to the Maroon Lake parking lot and arrived back at the car at 10:10 p.m. We were proud to have climbed these mountains! Next and final stop, Snowmass. Double thanks, Bill Arnold!

To quote Bill Arnold:

"...The Smiths...have learned to help each other on the mountain when help is needed. This is a very good thing on a climb. Another thing that impressed me was their toughness. Whether the difficulty was a technical one, or bad weather, or personal discomfort, they have learned to overcome it and get on with the climb. I was proud to be associated with this family."

"It doesn't cost anything to say 'Thanks.'"
G. NASH SMITH

Photo 110 – Rappel practice, getting ready to climb the Bells (from left: Flint, Cody, Tyle) 1968

Photo 111 – Hiking with Kay Arnold to Crater Lake

Photo 112 – Traversing on North Maroon Peak July 13, 1968

Photo 113 – Working a couloir

Photo 114 – On top of North Maroon (from left: Bill Arnold, Tyle, Flint, Quade, Cody) July 13, 1968

Photo 115 – Tyle downclimbing between the Bells

Photo 116 – Flint chose to rappel instead of downclimbing

Photo 117 – On the way to Maroon Peak

Photo 118 – On top of Maroon Peak (from left: Bill Arnold, Quade, Flint, Cody, Tyle) July 13, 1968

Photo 119 – Heading down

Photo 120 – Working a wall

Photo 121 – Roping up to descend the Maroon Peak snow couloir (from left: Flint, Tyle, Cody, Bill)

Photo 122 – Good snow conditions in the couloir

Chapter 20

Colorado Finale!

Yee Haah! We're practically there! It was Sunday, July 14, 1968, and we were backpacking to Snowmass Lake at the base of Snowmass Mountain, our final Colorado 14er (see photos 123-125)! We set up camp by the beautiful lake in this pristine area and enjoyed a pleasant evening around our campfire. Tomorrow would not be just another day. I was excited and anxiously anticipating the climb. I felt nostalgic. I am not sure the boys felt the same way. For me it was the end of an era. Snowmass represented the wonderful culmination of a monumental family goal to climb all 53 of Colorado's 14ers.

On July 15, 1968, we made our ascent of Snowmass Mountain. And guess what? Happy 16th Birthday, Flint! Quade was 12, Cody 11, and Tyle 8. It was a spectacular day on a beautiful peak. We were amazed at the amount of snow remaining in mid-July. Part way up we crossed paths with two men from the Aspen area who had just summited Snowmass. We visited for a while and they took a couple of photos for us. It turned out that one of them had connections with the Aspen Times newspaper and would write an article about us (see photo 126 and Appendix 3).

We enjoyed climbing Snowmass a great deal and savored the day! We took our time and played in the snow, reaching the summit after four hours. We took pictures and ate lunch, spending a whole hour on top. What a special day (see photo 127)! There was no reason to rush. We took it all in and the boys started to grasp what we had accomplished. It took an hour and a half to get back to camp, another hour to gather our gear and then four hours to hike to the trailhead. We were pleased with our accomplishment. We had done what we set out to do. Tyle, age 8, was now the youngest person to have climbed all the Colorado 14ers (see photos 128, 129). The boys and I had enjoyed wonderful experiences together and had memories that would last a lifetime. I felt some sadness that this journey was over.

My sister, Dorothy, was so impressed with what we had done that she contacted *The Denver Post,* who sent Cal Queal to our house to interview us. He wrote an article titled, "The Saga of the Climbing Smiths," that appeared in *Empire Magazine* on October 13, 1968. That's how we got our name (see photo 130 and Appendix 4).

"Rather than follow in someone's footsteps,
I prefer to make my own."
G. NASH SMITH

"4 plus 1 = 53."
G. NASH SMITH

Photo 123 – Snowmass Mountain trailhead (from left: Tyle, Cody, Quade, Flint) July 14, 1968

Photo 124 – Beaver dam crossing heading to Snowmass Lake

Photo 125 – Snowmass Mountain from Snowmass Lake

Photo 126 – Below the summit of Snowmass Mountain, our final Colorado 14er (from left: Cody, George, Tyle, Flint, Quade)

Photo 127 – Celebrating on the summit of Snowmass Mountain
(from left: Flint, Cody, Quade, Tyle) July 15, 1968

Photo 128 – At "The Outpost" celebrating our success in climbing all the Colorado 14ers
(from left: Quade Tyle, Flint, George, Cody, Mocha), Tyle had just popped out of Flint's backpack
to greet everyone 1968

Photo 129 – Bob Melzer, the prior record holder, congratulating Tyle on becoming the youngest person to have climbed all the Colorado 14ers 1968

Photo 130 – The five Smiths plus Mocha, photo taken by Cal Queal, writer for The Denver Post 1968

Chapter 21

Mocha D Smith

We always had a dog, or two or three, but there was only one like Mocha. In 1960 I was a Real Estate Salesman for Monte Carroll & Company. I was working with a customer looking for farmland in the Brighton area, north of town. At one of the listings, the farmer had a litter of pups he had to get rid of because he was going to move. So, I brought one home.

The subject of getting a puppy had been discussed for several months by Flint and Quade. They were already doing chores around the house to earn an allowance, but Marilou and I devised a plan where they could earn extra points towards getting a puppy. This puppy was such an immediate success that we talked about getting a second one. When I went back to that farm later in the week, I sadly found out that the rest of the litter had been put to sleep.

Mocha, as she would come to be named, was an Australian Sheep Dog who acted like we were her flock. And she enjoyed the mountains. She didn't need to be on a leash. When we were spread out while hiking, she thought her job was to patrol us from front to back, counting her flock. After each climb we would stop for a victory meal at a Dairy Queen or similar-style restaurant, that included ice cream, and Mocha was rewarded with a vanilla cone of her own.

She was ambidextrous, but that's not the right word for it. If there was another dog in the area where we stopped that needed to take a leak, she would duplicate the action. If it was a female, she would squat. If it was a male, she would lift her leg.

Over the years, Mocha scaled 30 of the 14ers, some of them were considered difficult, including Lindsey, Little Bear, Blanca, Wetterhorn, and Snowmass. Plus, she climbed 8 repeats. Flint designed a custom harness for her made out of webbing that was stitched at a shoe repair shop. To get her used to the harness, we practiced raising and lowering her from the second-floor balcony of our house. After that, Mocha seemed to understand that if we put her in a harness it was for her own good. Sometimes, on a ridge, she would lower her center of gravity before proceeding for added safety when there was exposure.

Mocha had great route-finding ability, and could move fluidly even in rocky terrain. Yet she had the patience and good sense to let us lift her to get her over a tricky section. She didn't whimper or balk, even during long, difficult days, or during bad weather.

On a trip to climb Pikes Peak in October, 1966, we had other dogs with us. Along with Mocha, we brought Freckles and Princess. Soon after we started, a porcupine showed up. While Mocha stayed back, Freckles and Princess got a muzzle full of quills. Mocha wanted nothing to do with the porcupine and was the only dog we took on a climb after that. Mocha did get sprayed by a skunk once, but only once, not so for our other dogs.

She was truly a member of The Outpost Mountain Club and a price-less part of our family. She was a unique mountain climbing dog and provided lots of happiness for us (see photos 131-139). Table 1 includes all of the first-time 14er climbs she made, four of which took place after 1969 (see Mocha Climbs, Table 1).

"Who wants to go climbing?" "Woof!"
G. NASH SMITH

Photo 131 – On our way up Grays Peak (from left: Cody, Mocha, Flint, Quade) July 17, 1965

Photo 132 – Grays Peak summit ("Mocha, you knucklehead, get under the tarp") July 17, 1965

Photo 133 – On a Pikes Peak attempt October 1966

Photo 134 – Mocha at home 1967

Photo 135 – Mocha leading the way to Mt. Belford October 1, 1967

Photo 136 – On San Luis Peak after Tyle fell into the creek June 9, 1968

Photo 137 – Mocha roped up on Mount Lindsey June 21, 1968

Photo 138 – Feeding Mocha a victory ice cream cone 1968

Photo 139 – Mocha congratulating Tyle 1969

MOCHA CLIMBS

14er	Mtn Name	Date	14er	Mtn Name	Date
1	Mt. Lincoln	9/6/1964	16	Culebra Peak	7/23/1967
2	Mt. Bross	9/6/1964	17	Mt. Holy Cross	8/27/1967
3	Grays Peak	7/17/1965	18	Missouri Mtn.	9/24/1967
4	Mt. Yale	8/28/1965	19	Mt. Belford	10/1/1967
5	Mt. Democrat	8/15/1966	20	Mt. Oxford	10/1/1967
6	Mt. Columbia	8/20/1966	21	San Luis Peak	6/9/1968
7	Quandary Peak	9/10/1966	22	Mt. Harvard	6/15/1968
8	Mt. Shavano	9/25/1966	23	Mt. Sherman	6/16/1968
9	Tabeguache Peak	9/25/1966	24	Mt. Lindsey	6/21/1968
10	Pikes Peak	6/3/1967	25	Little Bear Peak	6/23/1968
11	Mt. Antero	6/10/1967	26	Blanca Peak	6/23/1968
12	Mt. Sneffels	7/2/1967	27	Wetterhorn Peak	7/4/1970
13	Handies Peak	7/6/1967	28	Uncompahgre Peak	7/4/1970
14	Redcloud Peak	7/7/1967	29	Torreys Peak	7/25/1970
15	Sunshine Peak	7/7/1967	30	Snowmass Mtn.	8/26/1971

TABLE 1

Chapter 22

HEADING WEST

In the fall of 1968, I thought of a new family climbing challenge for me and the boys. We had climbed all of Colorado's 14ers but what about the West Coast 14ers? I presented that idea to them. We talked about it and everyone said "yes." "Let's do it next summer." So, we began to make plans. There are thirteen 14ers in California, plus Mount Rainier in Washington, for a total of 14. The youngest person to climb these 14ers was, once again, Bob Melzer. He had finished them at age 11, in 1939, with his Dad, Carl.

The earliest I could get away in 1969 was August 10 and the boys had to be back by September 3 for the start of school. I had Flint plan the itinerary for our trip, including the order of mountains we would climb, suggested routes, and what gear and food we would need. Flint scheduled our trip to get us back on September 1, giving us a day to spare before the start of school.

Flint was not only our route finder, but also our technical leader. He studied a book called *Mountaineering: The Freedom of the Hills*, and other sources, to become more proficient in the use of technical gear, such as ropes, anchor setting, knot tying, and belaying.

Gerry Mountaineering learned of our trip and thought it would be a good chance for them to test some equipment, so they outfitted us with backpacks and sleeping bags. We looked forward to using lightweight down sleeping bags for the first time. They would be a big improvement compared to the heavier flannel bags we were used to when backpacking. Up until this point we didn't have any state-of-the-art gear. We hiked in blue jeans, cotton tee-shirts and sweatshirts. Our most functional items were wool sweaters. Cody had outgrown his favorite red sweater and Tyle inherited it this summer. We finished the Colorado 14ers with construction boots but had upgraded to Vibram-soled boots for the Sierras. Flint bought dehydrated meals, pre-packaged lunches and other necessary equipment mainly from Holubar Mountaineering, Inc. He had to figure out how to get all of our gear and food for twenty-three days loaded into the 1966 blue Ford Fairlane station wagon and still have room for five people. That took some doing. Besides our dehydrated dinners and breakfasts for our backpacking trips, we also had lunch items, including space food sticks, dried fruit, candy bars, beef jerky and pre-packaged trail lunches. I had Sinclair, Texaco, Husky, Shell and Continental Oil gas station credit cards to buy gas, and I had $215 cash to take. That money would be used to pay for incidentals, such as laundry, fresh fruit, and once in a while we might splurge on a restaurant meal and a motel room. We started driving with Flint and me up front, Quade was in the second seat with some gear, and Cody and Tyle, being the smallest, were in the very back lying on un-rolled sleeping bags on top of equipment. Flint now had a driver's license and could share the driving.

It was early afternoon on August 10 when we headed west! I was age 41, Flint was 17, Quade 13, Cody 12, and Tyle was 10. The best route from Denver to the High Sierras at that time was over Berthoud Pass on U.S. Highways 6 and 40 (see photos 140-142). While driving we enjoyed listening to Mystery Theater and Denver Bears baseball when we could find either on the radio. We continued a ritual we had created on our Colorado climbs, which was to snack on Ritz crackers covered with Kraft Pimento cheese spread.

Just after one in the morning we stopped in Provo, Utah, and filled up with gas. We needed to decide whether to quit for the day or keep going. I had heard warnings about the temperature of the Nevada desert and asked the gas station attendant about it. He said, "It can get really hot." So, we chose to keep going to beat the heat. It was close to 5:30 a.m. when we got to Ely, Nevada, and gassed up again. The next available gas stop was 170 miles away, in Tonopah. We switched drivers and Flint drove for the first time. When we were about eighty miles west of Ely on Highway 6 the sun started to come up, warming the desert. Flint became drowsy and momentarily fell asleep at the wheel. Our vehicle drifted left off the highway, and Flint pressed hard on the brakes but the car kept going. It eventually did stop, though, when it hit a ditch about fifteen feet from a cement embankment (see photos 143, 144).

The wreck jostled us pretty good but everyone seemed to be okay. We got out to look at the damage. The front end and undercarriage were scraped and dented, and both front wheels had been forced outward and were "walleyed." We considered ourselves lucky, although we later found out I had a cracked rib and Cody a bruised sternum. We unloaded the car and took inventory of the food and equipment. Incredibly, the only damage we found was a broken bag of powdered milk. This was no doubt due to the good packing job Flint had done at the start of the trip.

The obvious question was, what's next? We for sure needed a tow. So, I would hitch a ride to the nearest town, Currant, find a phone and call for a tow truck out of Ely. I told the boys, "I might be gone for three hours. Flint, you are in charge." There wasn't much traffic in the early morning, but after a short while I thumbed a ride with a car going towards Ely. When we got to Currant, I saw a phone booth and asked the driver to stop. I thanked him for the ride and looked in the phone book for a tow company. I found Murdock's 24 Hour Towing out of Ely and called them. They said they would send a tow truck and pick me up on the way to the wreck. The tow truck picked me up at 9:30 a.m. and we drove to the accident (see photo 145). A Highway Patrolman was already there. Flint had been given a $25 citation for careless driving. The boys had reloaded our car and the tow driver hooked up our vehicle (see photo 146). We all crammed into the cab but when the tow truck pulled onto the highway our car's right rear tire went flat (you gotta be kidding me!). The tow truck driver unhooked our front end and hooked up our back end to lift the car so we could change the flat. We put on the spare (see photo 147). He then re-hooked to the front of our car, and we went to Ely.

At 12:30 p.m. our car was dropped off at the tow yard. It was assessed as a total loss. The tie rods were shot and the frame was bent (see photo 148). Now what? How do we get out of here? In this situation, most people would think, "We're done." But I'm not most people. This was obviously a setback and there could be more along the way, but I was determined to continue our trip. We needed a vehicle. There were two obvious choices, to rent a car or buy one. Curiosity had brought a small group of people around us and our wrecked car. I asked about car rentals, and it turned out there was one vehicle available that would cost $25 a day and twenty-five cents a mile. That was too much. Somebody else mentioned he thought Leo Curto had a car for sale and I should check with him. He pointed out Leo's office just two doors down. It turns out that Leo did have a 1953 Chevy wagon that he would sell for $250. I took it for a test drive and saw blue smoke coming out of the exhaust. He disclosed that the car needed a quart of oil every tankful of gas. I balked a little and he lowered the price to $225. I said, "I'll give you $200," and he said, "Okay." The car didn't have a safety inspection, license plates, or title, and I needed all my cash. We shook hands on a seemingly nothing-for-nothing trade. Leo gave me a bill of sale and I gave him an IOU. I promised I would have my wife send him a check and we transferred the license plates from our Ford to the Chevy.

"If you say you'll do something, do it.
There is nothing more sacred than a man's word."
G. NASH SMITH

This ordeal tested our resolve. We loaded our gear into "Alan Ohlsen," as the Chevy came to be called. Alan Ohlsen was a Norwegian climber whose name we saw on a summit register earlier that summer. For some reason that name stayed with me and seemed appropriate for our new vehicle (see photo 149).

It was obvious that Flint felt a tremendous sense of guilt because of the car wreck (see photo 150). But I had always tried to instill in the boys that we were a team and would stick together no matter what happens. Tyle wondered if the wreck was a bad omen and whether we should go on. I gathered the boys together and said, "We're not done yet. We hit a big bump in the road but we're okay. Let's see if we have what it takes to beat what's ahead. For us to reach our goal, it's not *if* we continue, 'cause we're gonna, but *how* we respond to the challenges that might show up along the way."

We had wrecked a car, bought a used one and were about to leave Ely and continue our trip. And if we climb a mountain tomorrow we will still be on schedule. An eventful day, for sure!

"I've been in tougher places than this,
I just can't remember when."
G. NASH SMITH

Photo 140 – About to start our West Coast climbing trip, Mocha was sad she would not be going along (from left: Cody, Flint, George, Quade, Mocha, Tyle) on day 1; August 10, 1969

Photo 141 – US Highway 40

Photo 142 – Berthoud Pass (from left: Cody, Flint, Tyle, Quade)

Photo 143 – We drifted off the highway on day 2; August 11, 1969

Photo 144 – Unpacking the car (from left: Cody, Tyle, Flint, Quade) lucky we missed the culvert

Photo 145 – Nevada Highway Patrol car and Murdock's tow truck

Photo 146 – Getting hooked up

Photo 147 – Flat rear tire, darn it

Photo 148 – Our station wagon was totaled

Photo 149 – Loading up our new transportation, a 1953 Chevy (from left: Flint, Quade, Cody, Tyle)

Photo 150 – With "Alan Ohlsen", our newly acquired station wagon
(from left: George, Quade, Cody, Tyle, Flint) on day 2; August 11, 1969

Chapter 23

ISN'T THIS FUN, JIMMY?

We left Ely, Nevada, in our newly acquired, old vehicle and drove late into the night. At 1:30 a.m. we found a wide spot off of Highway 6 in Owens Valley, four miles before the town of Bishop, California, where we slept (see photo 151). It turned out Alan Ohlsen burned more than a little oil. So, we ended up buying a case of oil and settled into a routine of adding two quarts every 100 miles, plus switching drivers. The events of the last two days had left us short on sleep. But we pressed on and were able to get to the Tuttle Creek trail for our Mount Langley climb late Tuesday morning, August 12. The Tuttle Creek trail started at 6,300 feet in elevation and after hiking forty-five minutes we came upon the Tuttle Creek Ashram (a stone and concrete structure in the shape of a cross), at 7,600 feet. We still had another 6,500 feet to gain, and that was too much. We didn't have enough time because of our late start. So, we went back to the car. Now, in order to try and keep on schedule to climb something today, we opted to do White Mountain. White Mountain has less total elevation to gain, and there is a road all the way to the top that we can hike on. We could finish in the dark, if we had to.

From Tuttle Creek we drove about ninety miles to the White Mountain Trailhead, passing through the Ancient Bristlecone Pine Forest, which contains the oldest-living bristlecone pine trees in the world. One of these trees is known to be over 4,700 years old. The branches of these trees are twisted, gnarly, and quite beautiful.

We arrived at a closed gate at 11:30 a.m. and began the seven-mile hike to the top of White Mountain (see photos 152-154). After two miles we passed the White Mountain Research Center (WMRC) at 12,500 feet. There was an interesting looking research station on top but we didn't want to take the time to explore it. We signed the register, took a photo (see photo 155), got back to the car at 7 p.m. and drove back towards Mount Langley. We had climbed a 14er so we were still on schedule. We got to Lone Pine after midnight and slept a few miles outside of town on the side of the road.

*Photo 151 – Waking up near the Owens River Bridge on the way to
Mount Langley on day 3; August 12, 1969*

Photo 152 – Ready for White Mountain (from left: Tyle, Flint, Quade, Cody)

Photo 153 – Start of White Mountain Peak

Photo 154 – Hiking towards White Mountain August 12, 1969

Photo 155 – View south off the top of White Mountain Peak

On day four of the trip we got up and drove eight miles to the Tuttle Creek trailhead again (see photo 156). Flint and Cody decided to wear shorts because of the August heat. After reaching the Ashram we started on a trail but soon had to bushwhack to get above timberline. This didn't seem to be a popular route. In fact, we found no evidence of any other hikers (see photo 157).

Due to the heat, we needed to ration water early. Once above timberline we encountered a series of stubby rocks, different from any we had seen before. They were basically flat on top with oval-shaped indentations that collected rain. We were excited to have found drinking water. Each of us chose a small pool to sample. *Pitooey*, we spit it out. It turns out the water was stagnant and tasted awful. After that experience, we had a family joke. When we came across lousy-tasting water, we would chuckle and remark, "Ugh. This tastes like Langley water."

Because of the bushwhacking, the steepness of the route and the elevation gain, this climb was taking us a long time. We had made our way up to a ridge and were following it west to the summit (see photo 158). Flint and I left our packs near a memorable rock formation to lighten our load and we all hustled to the top (see photo 159). It was turning dark when we summited, so we didn't stay long. To save time on the way down it looked best to cross a snowfield. While traversing, Tyle slipped and slid about fifty feet down the slope, using his hands to help him stop. He called out and we quickly descended to him and I helped him warm his hands. He was okay.

Even though we had a flashlight, the memorable rock formation where we left our packs was not as memorable in the dark. It took a while to locate our packs. We finally got down to timberline. There were thorny thistles everywhere. The thistles were painful, especially for Flint and Cody, who had bare legs. We became increasingly annoyed about the situation and in the midst of our frustration, I blurted out, "Isn't this fun, Jimmy?" The boys looked at me and started to laugh. And thus, an imaginary friend of the family named "Jimmy" was born. The discomfort somehow was less, and Jimmy became an invisible member of our climbing family.

Jimmy was incredible. He never complained. He was strong and silent. In fact, he never uttered a word. But he was a kid who found joy in every aspect of our climbs. He was full of optimism. He only showed up when we were not having any fun. We could always count on Jimmy to help us get through the tough times.

We were exhausted and a long way from the car, so, we quit for the night. We found a pine tree that could provide some shelter and slept next to it. A couple of the boys fit under its branches. The next morning, we watched the sunrise and then bushwhacked down past the Ashram (see photos 160, 161) and returned to Alan Ohlsen.

We were scheduled to climb Mount Muir and Mount Whitney today but our night on Langley fouled that up. We could really use a good night's sleep so we got a room at the Dow Villa Motel in Lone Pine. Two of us slept on the bed and three on the floor. We took showers, did our laundry, shopped for candy bars and oranges, called home, and went to the ranger station to get the required overnight permit to be in the Whitney backcountry, which we would use starting tomorrow. We were five days into this trip and already a day behind.

That night we found a restaurant called BoBo's Bonanza. They had a good-looking menu. Everyone enjoyed their meal and I agreed that the food tasted really good. It was so good we talked about coming back after climbing the Whitney group.

"I may need to juggle priorities today. I may feel overwhelmed today. I may get discouraged today. But quit? Not today."
G. Nash Smith

Photo 156 – Getting ready to climb Mount Langley on day 4

Photo 157 – Heading for Mount Langley

Photo 158 – Resting on a ridge late in the day

Photo 159 – Quade getting close to the summit of Mount Langley August 13, 1969

143

Photo 160 – Going down after a night of bivouacking, day 5; August 14, 1969

Photo 161 – Nearing the Ashram

Chapter 24

VISIONS OF BOBO'S

Following are Quade's recollections, with input from everyone else, about climbing the five 14ers that make up the Whitney group. They are: Mounts Muir, Whitney, Russell, Tyndall and Williamson. Mount Whitney is the tallest 14er in the contiguous forty-eight states, with an elevation of 14,494 feet. See the Mount Whitney group topographical maps at the end of this chapter for our route on these peaks.

After a good night's sleep at the Dow Villa Motel in Lone Pine we started driving west to the Whitney Portal, at an elevation of 8,374 feet (see photo 162). Our plan was to backpack, carrying all the equipment we thought we would need and food for three days to climb all five mountains. On the first day, we would backpack seventeen miles and gain 8,500 feet in elevation, climb Mounts Muir and Whitney, and continue north past Mount Russell to set up camp at Wallace Lake. The second day, we would leave our backpacks at Wallace Lake and climb Mounts Tyndall and Williamson in a loop, hike fifteen miles and gain 7,000 feet in elevation, and return to our Wallace Lake camp that same day. On the third day we would break camp and climb Mount Russell on our way back to the car. That day's effort would require twelve miles of hiking and a gain of 2,600 feet.

On Friday, August 15, 1969, our sixth day from home, we began backpacking the eleven-mile trail to Mount Whitney (see photos 163-166). Several miles up the trail, one particularly steep section zigzags back and forth ninety-nine times as it gains altitude, and ends at Trail Crest, elevation 13,777 feet (see photos 167, 168). When we got there, it was 4 p.m. We hiked north about a third of a mile to a cairn that marked the start of the climb up Mount Muir. We met Bob Mount on the summit of Muir at 5 p.m. and spoke with him for a few minutes (see photos 169, 170).

To quote Bob Mount:

"...once a year I make my pilgrimage to Whitney Portal and try for the wearying summit. I've been on Whitney twice, but my favorite climb there is Mt. Muir.... It's perhaps one of the clearest views for 360-degrees of scenery in the Sierras, because of its sharp summit.... I was sitting on the summit enjoying the sun and the view, and browsing through the Sierra Club log last summer when I heard voices... Children's voices... and I wondered where it might be coming from. I looked over the nearby summits and saw a teenaged boy standing at the brink of the east face above the Portal, looking my way. So far, not so unusual. Then a smaller boy appeared. After much shouting, another still smaller boy appeared. And finally, a fourth, the smallest of all, who appeared to be perhaps 10.... Anyway, the older boy, who turned out to be Flint Smith, 17, was scrambling up the final ascent even before his father appeared with the others.... I was alarmed about the small fry, and thought perhaps here were some nuts from Los Angeles that didn't know what they were doing. I told Flint it was a bit rough for the smaller boys, didn't he agree? Then I got the word about the Smith family and its adventures... and was so shook by their accomplishments I forgot to ask their advice on certain climbing matters! I enjoyed the brief visit with them, and greatly admire their father for what he has undertaken and accomplished."

We said goodbye to Bob and went back down to the trail and continued on to the summit of Mount Whitney, getting there at 7 p.m. California has a lot of beautiful sunsets (see photo 171).

There is a stone shelter on top of Mount Whitney where climbers can spend the night. But by the time we arrived the spaces had been claimed, so we camped outside. Since we did not get to Wallace Lake today we were further behind schedule.

Photo 162 – Road to Whitney Portal, Mount Whitney is on the left

Photo 163 – Hiking the Mount Whitney trail on day 6 from home and day 1 for the Whitney group
(from left: Cody, Tyle, Quade, Flint) August 15, 1969

Photo 164 – Rest stop on the Mount Whitney trail (from left: Flint, Quade, Cody, Tyle)

Photo 165 – Looking back towards Whitney Portal

Photo 166 – View towards Mount Muir while nearing Trail Crest

Photo 167 – Flint at Trail Crest

Photo 168 - Great view of Hitchcock Lakes (from left: Flint, Tyle, Quade, Cody)

Photo 169 – Cody and Tyle prepare to make a final scramble to the summit of Mount Muir (on the right out of picture) with Mount Whitney in the background

Photo 170 – Top of Mount Muir (from left, George, Flint, Tyle, Cody, Quade) note Tyle wearing Cody's red sweater used on Colorado climbs August 15, 1969

Photo 171 – Sunset from the top of Mount Whitney

After a chilly night, we had a hot breakfast, packed up, and went on our way (see photos 172-174). We started down Mount Whitney's massive west face at 8:30 a.m. and then descended north on a rocky ridge into the basin between Whitney and Russell. From there we crossed in front of Russell and gained the ridge on its east side (see photos 175-177). We decided to change our plan and not go directly to Wallace Lake but climb Mount Russell now instead of on our way out. We left our backpacks on the ridge at 2 p.m. and headed up. The route was steep and involved some exposed ridge climbing.

Mount Russell is well off the beaten path. It has breathtaking exposure and even the standard route requires continuous use of hands (see photos 178-180). We got to the summit at 4:15 p.m. and found what to our surprise was the original register, placed there by Norman Clyde in 1926! Because of that find, we thought it must be the least-climbed 14er in the contiguous forty-eight states. What a spectacular mountain (see photo 181)!

Because it was getting late, we only spent a few minutes on top then headed down to our backpacks on the east ridge. We rethought our plan. We would take our gear down to the saddle, stash most of it nearby and go light to Wallace Lake to spend the night, ready to climb two peaks the next day. Flint and Dad would take daypacks, with a few items of clothing, our tent, water, one day's worth of trail snacks, and some hard candies. I would take the rope (see photo 182). Tomorrow we would blitz Tyndall and Williamson, retrieve our backpacks and hike out. If we could do that, we would still meet our three-day schedule for the group.

We got to Wallace Lake at 7:45 p.m. and spent a cold night in the tent without sleeping bags.

Photo 172 – Morning photo of Cody preparing to take down the tent atop Mount Whitney with Mount Langley in the background on day 2 in this group

Photo 173 – Tyle and Flint near Mount Whitney shelter

Photo 174 – Top of Mount Whitney the morning after summiting
(from left: Tyle, George, Quade, Flint, Cody) August 16, 1969

Photo 175 – Mount Russell

Photo 176 – Crossing over to Russell

Photo 177 – Working our way up to the east ridge of Mount Russell

Photo 178 – Looking back to Mount Whitney

155

Photo 179 – On the east ridge of Mount Russell after leaving our backpacks

Photo 180 – Continuing up the ridge to Mount Russell

156

Photo 181 – Top of Mount Russell (from left: Tyle, Quade, Cody, Flint) August 16, 1969

Photo 182 – Heading for Wallace Lake after stashing our backpacks on the ridge

In the morning we looked at the topographical map. We had to choose between walking more miles or gaining more elevation on our route to Tyndall (see photo 183). If we chose the mileage option, we would drop down to the John Muir trail and follow it in a big arc for several miles before climbing Tyndall. The elevation option would be to head more directly to Tyndall but required crossing several ridges. It turns out we came up with a third choice. We left Wallace Lake at 8:30 a.m. and ended up traversing horizontally where we could but tried to keep heading directly towards Tyndall. Soon after we started we passed by some fishermen and campsites along the lake. These were the first people we had seen since we left the summit of Mount Whitney. We worked our way to where we could see our route up Tyndall (see photos 184, 185).

We finally got to the base and started up. The route involved ascending a massive scree slope that sapped our strength. Each step required extra work. At one point Dad paused, took a deep breath and hollered, "Isn't this fun, Jimmy?" Despite our agony, his timing was perfect! Everyone laughed and cheered up a bit and we pushed on to the summit, getting there a little after 4 p.m. (see photo 186). It was late in the day, we were really beat and had already eaten most of our food. Our plan to make quick work of these two peaks, get back to our packs, and out to the car was not going to happen. It turns out we would not even get Williamson today. Our new plan was to just do what we could do.

So, in the late afternoon, we headed east down steep slabs into the Williamson bowl, located between the two peaks. It started to rain lightly but there was no place to set up our tent in the moraine of rocks. We had the good fortune to find an opening in the rocks that resembled a foxhole big enough for all of us to drop down into. We draped the tent over the opening like a tarp to create a roof.

The rain began to fall harder. Our tent fabric kept us dry for a while, but eventually we got soaked. We had few options available to make our situation better. We finished the rest of our food but were still hungry, and tired, and cold, and wet. Then someone mentioned Bobo's and we began to reminisce. Thinking about BoBo's gave us something to look forward to and helped to distract us from our discomfort.

Photo 183 – Wallace Lake camp, the morning of day 3 in this group August 17, 1969

Photo 184 – View back to Mount Russell (center) and Mount Whitney (far right)

Photo 185 – View to Mount Tyndall and scree slope

Photo 186 – On the summit of Mount Tyndall with Mount Williamson in the distance (from left: Cody, Flint, Tyle, Quade) August 17, 1969

The next morning it had cleared up and we dried the tent in the sun (see photo 187). Flint reviewed *A Climber's Guide to the High Sierra* as to how to climb Mount Williamson, which loomed before us like a maze of small pyramids stacked on top of one another with couloirs on each side.

We began hiking towards Williamson at 9 a.m. The route finding was a bit more involved than on most of our previous climbs. We had to back-track more than once. It took time to figure out exactly which couloir to ascend. Needless to say, the climb up Mount Williamson took longer than we had planned (see photos 188-190).

It was 4:30 p.m. when we got to the summit (see photo 191) and we knew that we would not make it to our backpacks and sleeping bags that we'd left on Mount Russell. We were tired of sleeping in the cold without sleeping bags and wanted a campfire. We looked at the topo map to figure out where the closest trees might be and saw that they were at George Creek, which was several miles out of our way, but that's where we would go. We were gonna have a campfire! We followed the ridge down and talk-ed about BoBo's. Each of us shared what we would eat first, and second, and next. My list included chicken-fried steak, a BLT sandwich, meatloaf, and a chocolate shake. Boy, BoBo's sounded good. We got to George Creek around 7:30 p.m. and there was firewood. We built a fire and slept in a cir-cle around it. If someone woke he added wood to it. It was our third night in a row without sleeping bags, but the fire felt good. (see photos 192, 193).

Photo 187 – Drying our tent on rocks the morning after night 3 bivouac August 18, 1969

Photo 188 – Off route on Mount Williamson

Photo 189 – Oops, bad route choice

Photo 190 – Yeah! Mount Williamson's final couloir

Photo 191 – Top of Mount Williamson (from left: Cody, Flint, Tyle, Quade) August 18, 1969

Photo 192 – Heading down Mount Williamson

Photo 193 – Timberline camp near George Creek at sunset, day 4 in this group

After we put the fire out in the morning we confirmed the fastest route back to our packs would take us by Wallace Lake. We'd summited all five mountains but were another day behind schedule. We had no food, and were short on energy. We were running on fumes but had to get out of there. We started hiking at 9 a.m., hoping to get to Alan Ohlsen before the day was over. We went up to a notch on the east side of Mount Barnard and then dropped down a steep couloir into the Wallace Lake basin. We took extra caution during our descent because the rocks were loose and we were tired (see photo 194).

Photo 194 – View of Wallace Lake from notch on day 5 in this group August 19, 1969

As we approached Wallace Lake I kept an eye out for food of any kind that might have been left by one of the fishermen or campers we had seen a few days before. Cody saw a frog and we joked about our options if he caught it. We stopped to rest and Flint saw some plastic wedged between two rocks that he thought was probably trash. Dad had instilled in us the philosophy to "leave each day better than you found it," even by doing something as simple as picking up trash.

Flint grabbed it and, it wasn't trash after all. What do you know? It was a trail lunch! What are the odds? The frog was safe! The trail lunch had four shortbread cookies, a chocolate candy bar, a pemmican bar, a hard candy and some beef jerky. The challenge was to divide everything five ways. This little bit of food tasted good and was for sure a timely find. Just at that moment, Dad noticed a plane flying overhead. We were supposed to call home whenever we reached civilization. Since we were two days behind schedule, Dad wondered if Mom had instigated a search.

It was late afternoon when we trudged our way up the basin to pick up our backpacks that we had left three days earlier. Dad fell behind us and I heard him having "dry heaves." I asked if he was okay and he said he was.

We got to our backpacks. We were in a hurry to get to the car so we didn't want to take time to cook a full meal. We fired up the stove, and had soup and hot chocolate. It was nighttime but at least it was all downhill. We hiked over large slabs of granite rock that looked amazing and a bit eerie in the moonlight. We covered four miles and came to a cliff. Bummer. We could hear the North Fork of Lone Pine Creek below us but saw no obvious way down. Flint scouted and found a large tree leaning against the cliff that we used as an anchor for our rappel. We rappelled about forty feet to a small, raised area near the valley floor and then had a creek to cross.

Once on the ground we discovered yet another problem. We were surrounded by an army of thick willows that were ten feet tall. We could hear the nearby creek but even with the help of the flashlight we could not see it because of the willows, let alone cross it. At 9:30 p.m., we ended up calling it quits. How frustrating! We begrudgingly stamped down a small, bathtub-sized space and spent the night in the willows. There was no room for our down sleeping bags and we were afraid the willows would rip them anyway. Another night spent bivouacking, that made four in a row. We named this camp "Willow Heave" in honor of Dad's dry heaves and the willows.

The next morning, daylight made our route finding easier. We worked our way through the willows and across the creek. When we got on the Mount Whitney Trail it felt like we were walking on a highway. We got to the car at noon, took a photo, and loaded our gear. We were eager to get to Lone Pine (see photo 195). We were gonna buy some candy, rent a motel room, clean up, check in with Mom, and go to BoBo's.

When we got to BoBo's, Dad said we could eat whatever we wanted and as much as we wanted but cautioned us because our stomachs had shrunk. I was quite hungry and had a BLT, a meatloaf sandwich, and a chocolate milk shake. We took our time eating. We wanted to savor our first store-bought meal in six days (see photo 196). When we had had our fill, we returned to our room at the Dow Villa Motel. Dad was right, my stomach had shrunk and could not handle that much food. I hurried to the bathroom with an urge to throw up. Dad watched me and when he heard me retching, he hollered out, "Isn't that fun, Jimmy?" We all laughed. I laughed so much my sides hurt. We were proud to have finished climbing the Whitney group. In retrospect we were glad that our planned three-day trip only took us six days to complete! This was day eleven from home. We seemed to create our own hell but we survived it. Unfortunately, we were now four days behind schedule.

"Good judgment comes from experience.
Sometimes experience comes from bad judgment."
G. NASH SMITH

Photo 195 – Back at the car at Whitney Portal
(from left: Cody, Tyle, Quade, Flint, George) on day 6 in this group August 20, 1969

Photo 196 – Outside BoBo's Restaurant Lone Pine
(from left: Cody, Flint) day 11 from home August 20, 1969

MOUNT WHITNEY GROUP MAPS

Mt. Whitney 1956 & Lone Pine 1958 USGS Topographical Maps

Maps 1-4: Route of our 6 day, 5 night trip from August 15-20, 1969

LEGEND:
Number indicates day/night in this group

SOD	Start of Day
1	Camp with sleeping bags
2, 3, 4, 5	Bivouac-no sleeping bags, night 2 with tent
2, 5	Backpacks-drop off or pick up
1, 2, 3, 4	Peak summited on day listed
←	Our route-dark pencil marks were made in 1969
	Note: An "x" on the route marks our sleeping bag, bivouac, or backpack drop off or pick up location

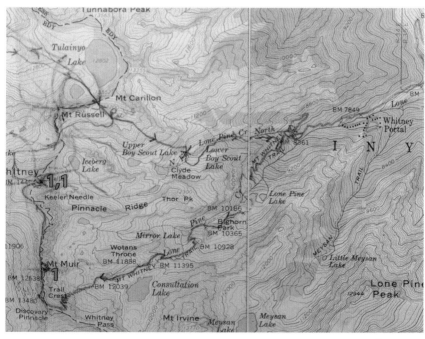

Map 1 SOD day 1 Whitney Portal; To Mount Muir & Mount Whitney summits **1***,*
camp on Mount Whitney summit **1**

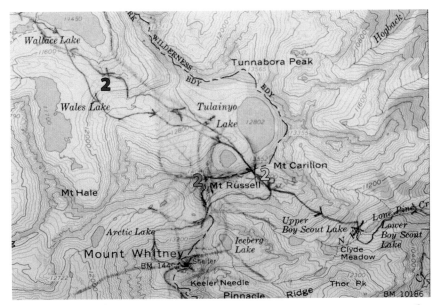

Map 2 SOD day 2 Top of Mount Whitney; SOD day 2 Top of Whitney to Mount Russell summit **2**,
To drop packs on Mount Russell ridge 2, *To Wallace Lake bivouac night* **2**

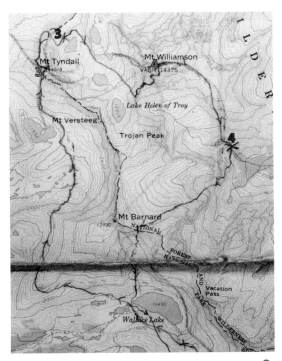

Map 3 SOD day 3 Wallace Lake; To Mount Tyndall summit **3**,
To Mount Tyndall bivouac **3**, *SOD day 4 Mount Tyndall bivouac; To Mount Williamson summit* **4**,
To George Creek bivouac **4**, *SOD day 5 George Creek*

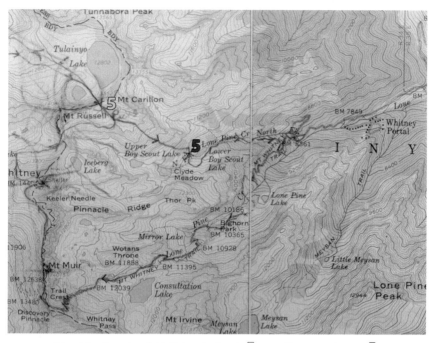

Map 4 day 5 continued; To Pick up backpacks ⑤, *To Willow Heave bivouac* **5**,
then out to car at Whitney Portal day 6, August 20, 1969

Chapter 25

Fantastic! Fantastic!

Following are Cody's recollections, with input from everyone else, about climbing the five 14ers that make up the Palisade group. See the Palisade group topographical maps at the end of this chapter for our route on these peaks.

The Palisades are considered to have the three most challenging 14ers in California, namely North and Middle Palisade, and Thunderbolt. According to what we had read and heard, all three of these peaks would be more technically challenging than any of the 14ers in Colorado. Mount Sill and Split Mountain are the other two 14ers in this range.

As we recuperated in our Dow Villa Motel room in Lone Pine, we talked about what had gone wrong in the Whitney group. Climbing that cluster of five peaks was different than anything we had done in Colorado. It involved carrying more equipment, gaining more elevation and hiking more miles than on any group of Colorado 14ers. Not even the four peaks in the Crestone group or the three Needle Mountains require such an extensive backpacking trip. In the Whitney group we had misjudged distances and elevation gain and underestimated the effort involved in carrying full packs. Much of the mileage covered was cross-country, often slow-going, over tricky terrain. In addition, the extreme heat and dryness added to the challenge.

Flint's research into the routes in the Palisades resulted in a more realistic itinerary. Because of their technical nature, his plan called for seven days to climb these five peaks. The first day we would backpack fifteen miles from South Lake to Palisade Lakes and camp. The next two days we would climb Split Mountain and Middle Palisade, and move our camp to the north. We would climb the remaining three peaks over the next three days, then pack out on day seven. We envisioned having a comfortable tent camp each night, with sleeping bags, and plenty of food. No more bivouacking, we had done enough of that!

On the morning of August 21, day twelve from home, we checked out of our motel in Lone Pine and drove to Bishop to get the overnight permit needed for the Palisades. After eating a late lunch at the Bishop Burger House we drove to South Lake (see photos 197, 198). We had a week-long backpack trip ahead of us and needed to carry more stuff than ever. In addition to our normal gear, Flint had a 150-foot goldline rope and our technical equipment; namely carabiners, pitons, a hammer, and webbing. Quade had another rope and an ice axe.

At 5 p.m. we started hiking and by the time we got to Bishop Pass at 11,989 feet, it was dark. We kept going a few more miles until we found a clump of trees and decided to quit for the night, put out our sleeping bags at 10:45 p.m. and slept on the trail. So much for tent camping every night. We were at the edge of Dusy Basin and had covered approximately eight miles of the fifteen needed to get to Palisade Lakes.

Photo 197 – The Bishop Burger House

Photo 198 – Before heading into the Palisades from South Lake on day 12 from home and day 1 in the Palisade group August 21, 1969

We got up at 8 a.m. the next morning and took a first look at the terrain south of us. Everything was further away than we had hoped (see photo 199). The heavy weight of our full backpacks was again an issue. So, we changed our plan, which we had a lot of practice doing, and decided to shorten the distance we lugged our heavy loads and switch the order of mountains climbed. Instead of carrying our backpacks seven more miles towards Split Mountain, we decided to set up camp three miles from here near Barrett Lakes, and climb North Palisade and Sill first. Then the next day we would go light and climb the farther peaks, Middle and Split, and return to camp, which would be a lot of ground to cover. In order to get that done we would need an early start. An early start would be a first for us but we were willing to try it. Having decided on this change of plans, we took the time to cook a nice breakfast.

After breakfast, we packed up and left the trail at 10:30 a.m. and went cross-country through Dusy Basin over Knapsack Pass to Barrett Lakes (see photos 200, 201) and kept our eyes open for a suitable campsite. Trees were scarce so we looked for flat, grassy ground near water, and large rocks to shelter us from the wind. At 3:30 p.m. we settled on a spot between the two largest of the Barrett Lakes at approximately 11,600 feet (see photos 202, 203).

Photo 199 – Tree Camp at edge of Dusy Basin day 2 in the Palisade group

Photo 200 – Backpacking into Dusy Basin

Photo 201 – Taking a break at Knapsack Pass with a view of North Palisade Peak

Photo 202 – Barrett Lakes camp

Photo 203 – Rappel practice near Barrett Lakes camp (Flint rappelling and Tyle)

The next day, at 7:30 a.m., we set out to climb both North Palisade and Sill, intending to return to camp later that day. If there was an easy route up North Palisade, we didn't find it (see photos 204, 205). After gaining 1,000 feet on a rock moraine, the route involved steep couloirs with some 4ᵗʰ class rock climbing for an additional 1,600 feet. Our stomachs were still recovering from the famine-and-feast extravaganza at Bobo's after the Whitney group, and pitstops were frequent for more than one of us (see photo 206). There was rock fall danger and caution was required throughout. We used our hands a lot and our fingertips were becoming raw. Even so, we felt we were climbing well and got to the summit of North Palisade at 12:30 p.m. (see photos 207, 208).

To get to Mount Sill we chose to follow the ridge from North Palisade through the "U" notch (see photo 209). Down-climbing was very exposed but there was a handhold when you needed it. Dad had to be creative because the handholds were right-handed, and he mainly uses his left hand. We crossed the "U" notch and gained the ridge (see photo 210) and followed it to the summit (see photos 211-214). It was 5:45 p.m. by the time we got there. We ate what was left of our trail snacks and headed down.

We descended Mount Sill's Southwest Chute (see photo 215). Once we got into the basin we headed west and north over Potluck Pass. There was quite a bit of snow but the footing was good. We went over the pass and made our way to camp and got there at 9 p.m.

We cooked up a dehydrated meal and talked about the importance of getting an early start to climb Middle Palisade and Split Mountain tomorrow but couldn't decide how early was early enough. We jokingly said we would meet at 10 in the morning to discuss it. We got ready tonight for tomorrow's climb. Dad and Flint packed their daypacks with trail snacks, water and our extra clothing. Flint also packed our technical equipment and an ice axe. Quade would carry the goldline rope. Tyle and I would get off easy.

Photo 204 – Heading to North Palisade from Barrett Lakes camp day 3 in this group

Photo 205 – North Palisade

177

Photo 206 – Break time on North Palisade (blurred photo)

Photo 207 – Nearing the top

Photo 208 – Top of North Palisade (from left: Quade, Tyle, Flint, Cody) August 23, 1969

Photo 209 – Mount Sill from North Palisade prior to traversing

Photo 210 – Above the U notch heading to Mount Sill

Photo 211 – Ridge to Mount Sill (from left: Quade, Cody, Tyle)

Photo 212 – Heading to Mount Sill (from left: Flint, Quade, Cody, Tyle)

Photo 213 – Looking back toward North Palisade (center left) and Thunderbolt Peak (right)

Photo 214 – Mount Sill summit August 23, 1969

Photo 215 – Starting down Mount Sill

In the morning we got a 6:30 a.m. start, which was our earliest yet. We knew we had a big day ahead of us and would go as fast as we could, hoping to get back to camp this same day. We had plotted our course using topo maps and headed for Middle Palisade (see photo 216), hiking over Potluck Pass. Then we went cross-country, trying to maintain our elevation while hiking over several additional ridges, to 13,000 feet at the base of Middle Palisade. We'd covered about five miles and hadn't seen anyone else along the way. We felt alone in a vast wilderness. Looming above us was 1,000 feet of 4th class vertical blocks of white rock, which required technical skill. We ate some lunch and looked for our route. Some of us put on adhesive tape to protect our raw fingertips before starting this section. Flint led the way (see photos 217, 218).

After almost five more hours of climbing this steep section, and a couple of mistakes, we finally got to the top of Middle Palisade at 4:30 p.m. (see photos 219, 220). This took much longer than we had thought and we figured it would take as long to go down. Split Mountain was maybe four miles to the southeast as the crow flies but much further as the human walks. We wouldn't make it up Split today, but weren't returning to camp without it, so we adjusted our plan. We would bivouac tonight down in the valley, and tomorrow do Split and get back to our tent for dinner. Tonight, we would need to stretch our food and keep an eye out for water because there wasn't much left. Without a tent or sleeping bags we would sleep in the trees around a fire. It seemed like only last week we had done the same thing!

We carefully down climbed the 1,000 feet of steep rock walls. It actually took longer to go down than it did to go up. Below us we could see the John Muir Trail, which we would take over Mather Pass before detouring off to Split. But that was to be tomorrow's business. Now, we just needed to take advantage of the remaining daylight to get down another 1,500 vertical feet of tricky terrain to find a spot among the trees to build a fire and bivouac. It was 10 p.m. when we stopped at the first spot we liked, which turned out to be several hundred feet above the lake. We gathered wood and made a fire. There wasn't much food left for us to eat, just a couple of candy bars. We had a few lemon drops as well, and saved some of those for tomorrow. So much for stretching our food. Our canteens were nearly empty because we hadn't come across any fresh water on the descent. We could have kept going until we found water near the lake but we chose to stay put and get some sleep.

On the one hand we were hungry and it was chilly, and we didn't have sleeping bags. This suggests we wouldn't sleep well. On the other hand we were tired, having just finished a long, technically challenging day. This suggests we would sleep well. So, we curled around the campfire and, indeed, slept pretty well (see photo 221).

Photo 216 – Water break on the way to Middle Palisade, day 4 in this group

Photo 217 – Middle Palisade chimney

Photo 218 – Middle Palisade rock wall

Photo 219 – Middle Palisade summit (from left: Quade, Flint, Tyle, Cody) August 24, 1969

Photo 220 – View from Middle Palisade
(from left: North Palisade, Sill, with Norman Clyde Peak in foreground)

Photo 221 – Bivouac after Middle Palisade, morning of day 5

The next morning, we didn't have breakfast because there was nothing to eat. After the fire embers were put out with dirt, at 8:20 a.m. we started down towards the lake and hit the John Muir Trail. We were determined to get Split and return to our tented camp tonight, which would feel like a motel. Soon we came across a stream feeding the lake and drank our fill, then topped off our canteens. The trail was wide and we made good time up Mather Pass. It only took two hours (see photos 222, 223). When we got to the bottom of the pass, before heading cross-country to Split, we saw three backpackers coming towards us. Since we hadn't seen anyone for three days we waited and struck up a conversation with them. We met Arnold and Victor Steinhardt and their friend, Barbara Barkley, who were on an eight-day, 100-mile backpack trip and were headed to Palisade Lakes to camp tonight. They asked about us and we talked for a short while. They wondered how come we were so deep in the wilderness without backpacks, sleeping bags, or a tent. We explained the best we could and said our goodbyes.

We headed cross-country to Split Mountain, which was a few miles away. It was nice to climb an easy mountain for a change. Our fingers appreciated a day off from the coarse rock. We summited Split at 2:45 p.m., but didn't stay long, because we still were at least a dozen miles from our tent (see photos 224, 225).

We returned to the John Muir Trail and followed it back over Mather Pass, heading to Palisade Lakes. We came across a green canteen at a small stream crossing that looked like the one Arnold was drinking from earlier. We thought this was his and were hopeful that we could find him and return it. He had mentioned they planned to camp near a Palisade Lake but we didn't know which one. It was 6:30 p.m. and we were making good time, but still had about eight miles to go to get back to our tent (see photo 226).

As we got to the first Palisade Lake there were numerous tents and Dad began to call out in a loud voice, "Telegram for Arnold Steinhardt, Telegram for Arnold Steinhardt," hoping he would hear us. We went past the first lake with no Arnold to be found. Dad continued calling Arnold's name as we hiked the trail along the second lake. Lo and behold, near the mouth of the second lake, we saw Arnold waving his arms overhead. He had heard Dad calling and saw him holding up the canteen. Arnold hustled to meet us, crying out with exuberance, "Fantastic! Fantastic!" It was his canteen! We were all excited to have found each other.

Arnold asked us how far away our camp was and learned we still had about five miles to go. He and his team offered us some soup. We decided that rather than hike back to our tent in the dark we would gladly accept their offer. We learned that Arnold was the first violinist in the famous Guarneri String Quartet, an elite string-instrument ensemble based in New York City.

To quote Arnold Steinhardt:

"We met the Smiths on the final ascent to Mather pass. They were going the other way and as mountain people often do, we stopped to chat. You could tell immediately that they were no normal backpackers. There were no fancy clothes or complicated equipment and I had the feeling that Mr. Smith and his sons were not city people vacationing in the Mtns. but real natives. Of course this was confirmed to us later when they started up Mt. Sill with us. They were like so many mountain goats on the rocks.

"We were amazed to find out what the Smiths' project was, but after talking a while we parted company expecting never to see them again. We finally stumbled into camp that night at the lower end of Paradise (sic) Lake. I was tired and also mad because I had left my canteen halfway down the pass by a stream and didn't relish living like a camel for the rest of the trip.

"Picture our surprise to find the... Smith family... later that night – and one of them carrying my canteen at that. They had not been able to make it back to their campsite what with the darkness and so we drummed up a big pot of soup and yacked into the night."

We thanked them for dinner. Arnold was curious where we would sleep. We showed him a spot fifty yards away where we would have a campfire. We then gathered wood and said goodnight to Arnold. Then we made a fire and curled up around it (see photo 227).

Photo 222 – Trail to Mather Pass on day 5 in this group

Photo 223 – Flint with Split Mountain in the background

Photo 224 – Top of Split Mountain (from left: Flint, Quade, Tyle, Cody) August 25, 1969

Photo 225 – View from Split Mountain (from left: North Palisade, Mount Sill, Middle Palisade)

Photo 226 – Approaching Palisade Lakes

Photo 227 – Palisade Lakes bivouac, morning of day 6

The next morning, they were gonna climb Mount Sill and we were going to our camp, so at 9 a.m. we started walking together. Eventually, we said our goodbyes and parted ways (see photo 228). We agreed to come and see Arnold and his quartet when they next performed in Denver. Our route went cross-country over magnificent terrain with meadows, flowing streams, and of course a lot of big, white boulders.

We got back to our tent camp at 2:30 p.m. We were beat and a half. The first order of business was to have a good meal, so the stove was fired up and we ate some of our dehydrated dinners for lunch, which tasted pretty good. We had learned not to gorge ourselves. That afternoon we lounged around and enjoyed being lazy. We napped and later had dinner. We were early to bed and got a good night's sleep in our sleeping bags and tent.

Photo 228 – Smith kids with the Arnold Steinhardt trio (from left: Tyle, Cody, Quade, Flint, Arnold, Barbara, Victor) on day 6 in the Palisades

The next morning, we ate our first cooked breakfast in four days, consisting of dehydrated scrambled eggs and diced ham, then packed up our camp and set out for Thunderbolt at 9 a.m. (see photos 229, 230). We dropped our backpacks at Thunderbolt Pass, 12,800 feet, at 10:30 a.m., and shouldered up our technical gear for what we expected would be a long, hard climb (see photo 231). We started up the couloir on the unsteady rocks that were the norm for this range (see photo 232). At a certain point we heard voices above us and the hammering of pitons. Pitons are hard metal spikes pounded into cracks in the rock by a hammer for belaying purposes and climber safety. This was 1969, two years before major developments in climbing tools and equipment by Royal Robbins and Yvon Chouinard.

As we continued ascending the couloir, two climbers came into view above us that were using technical gear to climb up a vertical section. We moved to the wall on the right side of the couloir, and ascended there, following the advice of Virginia Nolan, who had climbed the Crestones with us. She was one of the first people to have climbed all the 14ers in the contiguous forty-eight states and had talked to us specifically about the route on Thunderbolt. After gaining about twenty-five feet on the wall we moved left, back into the center of the couloir, and continued up, being careful not to dislodge rocks on the climbers who were now below us. We learned the two climbers were Al Tooze and Fred Wing.

To quote Albert Tooze:
"On the morning of August 27, 1969, Fred Wing and I left our camp in Dusy Basin.... to climb Thunderbolt Peak via the Southwest Chute. After going over quite a section of scree and talus we were blocked by a narrow chimney choked with stones. We tried the chimney and made it with the protection of one pin to where the chute opened up above.

"About the time we were coiling up the rope there appeared the shock of our lives. Booming up over the edge off to the right from where we had came (sic) appeared four boys and a(sic) adult. Three of the boys looked too young for climbing and at first glance I thought the adult must have been out of his mind for bringing the boys up into as rough of going as this.

"I could have never been more wrong.... We exchanged a few words and introduced ourselves, finding the adult was the father of the four boys. George Smith and his sons, Flint, Quade, Cody, & Tyle.

"As we started on up George and his boys were soon far ahead of us.... The last I saw of them on the ascent was George going up the pitch from the notch on the crest."

After our brief visit with Al and Fred we continued ascending the couloir and before we knew it were looking east down to the Palisade Glacier. We had reached the top of the couloir at almost 14,000 feet. The route then moved up a vertical wall to the right of the couloir, to the summit. We found the wall climb to be short and the rock solid. I was first to have the pleasant surprise of arriving at the summit block at 12:30 p.m. I remember shouting to the others, "We have had our first stroke of good luck!"

Indeed, the climb was not as long or hard as we expected. In fact, it was enjoyable! We were very happy to be at the summit, and to have finished getting to the top of the fifth and final Palisade group 14er. The summit register of Thunderbolt is mounted about fifteen feet out of reach on a huge block of granite. Flint maneuvered his way up and then helped the rest of us touch the summit (see photos 233, 234). Eventually, Albert and Fred joined us on top and we continued talking with them.

Albert Tooze further wrote:
"They were nice enough to wait for us at the top where we took some pictures and Flint tossed the register down from the summit block and hung in the middle of nowhere while we signed it.

"After talking a bit we found out that George and his boys had only three (two) 14000+ foot peaks left to go in the continental United States. This made me feel quite humble, to share this peak with such and (sic) outstanding man and his devoted boys.

"George said that climbing had become almost a religion with him. I can only say that his religion will put a permanent bond between him and his boys from now on. This is a rarity in these mixed up times of today."

To quote Albert's climbing partner, Fred Wing:
"...I can't really tell you how it felt to meet you on the mountain. At first we were amazed, then humbled (to be so easily outclimbed by young boys), and finally we felt greater self-esteem because we felt a little bit as though we were part of your mission.

"...I was enormously impressed by you and your sons there on the mountain. You climbed with great skill, strength, intelligence and

courage. Your choice of a mission also manifested your wisdom about life-that great personal rewards come from giving yourself fully to something you cherish-the mountains, their challenge, and your acceptance of the challenge."

After our conversation we said goodbye and began a careful down-climb to our backpacks at Thunderbolt Pass.

At 3:30 p.m., we packed up, headed for Bishop Pass, then took the trail six more miles to South Lake and the car (see photos 235, 236). We got there at 7:45 p.m. Finally, we had a day when we felt we were moving pretty fast. We hadn't been setting any speed records in the Sierras. Well, maybe we had been for a group of five, comprised of one adult, two teenagers and two younger kids. That size of group has to be the comparison.

Our original plan was to spend seven days in the Palisades and in spite of itinerary changes along the way, that's how long it took us. We wanted to sleep in a tent camp every night but only did that three nights out of six.

We drove to Bishop, got a room at the Inyo Mono Inn, cleaned up, checked in with Mom, and spent the night. Tomorrow we'd head for Mount Shasta.

Photo 229 - Breaking camp, Barrett Lakes, on day 7 in this group

Photo 230 – On the way to Thunderbolt Pass (Thunderbolt Peak is far right)

Photo 231 – Dropping backpacks prior to climbing Thunderbolt Peak

Photo 232 – At the start of our route up Thunderbolt

Photo 233 – Cody on George's shoulders below the summit block

Photo 234 – Top of Thunderbolt Peak (from left: Tyle, Cody, Quade, George, Flint) August 27, 1969

Photo 235 – Rest break on Bishop Pass

Photo 236 – Final backpack, day 7 of the Palisade group August 27, 1969

PALISADE GROUP MAPS

Mount Goddard 1948 & Big Pine 1950 USGS Topographical Maps

Maps 5-8: Route of our 7 day, 6 night trip in the Palisade group from August 21-27, 1969

LEGEND:
Number indicates day/night in this group

SOD	Start of Day
1, 2, 3, 6	Camp with sleeping bags
4, 5	Bivouac-no sleeping bags
3, 4, 5, 7	Peak summited on day listed
←	Our route-dark pencil marks were made in 1969
	Note: An "x" on the route marks our sleeping bag, bivouac, or backpack drop off or pick up location

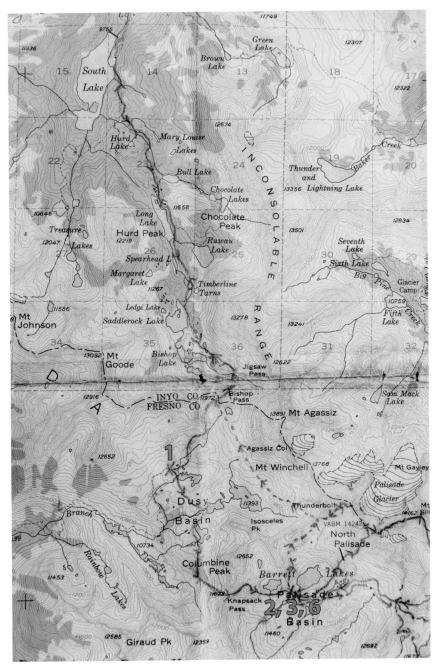

Map 5 SOD day 1 South Lake August 21, 1969; To Dusy Basin camp night **1**,
SOD day 2 Dusy Basin; To Barret Lakes camp nights **2**, **3**, **6**

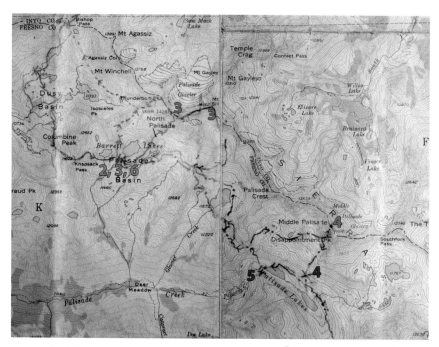

Map 6 SOD day 3 Barrett Lakes; To North Palisade summit **3**, To Mount Sill summit **3**, return To Barrett Lakes camp night **3**, SOD day 4 Barrett Lakes to Middle Palisade summit **4**, To Middle Palisade bivouac **4**

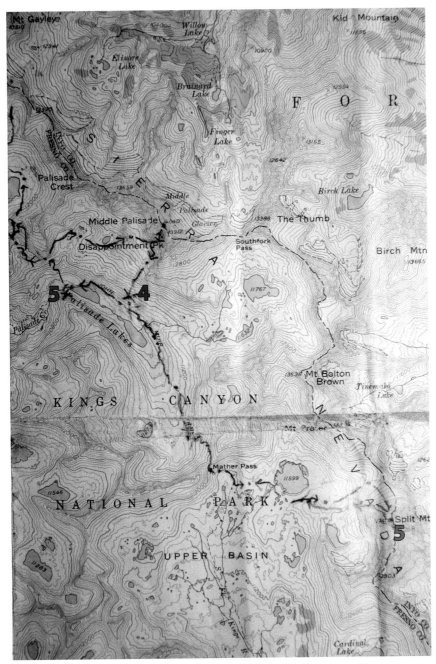

Map 7 SOD day 5 Middle Palisade bivouac; To Split Mountain summit 5,

To Palisade Lakes bivouac 5, SOD day 6 Palisade Lakes, To Barrett Lakes camp

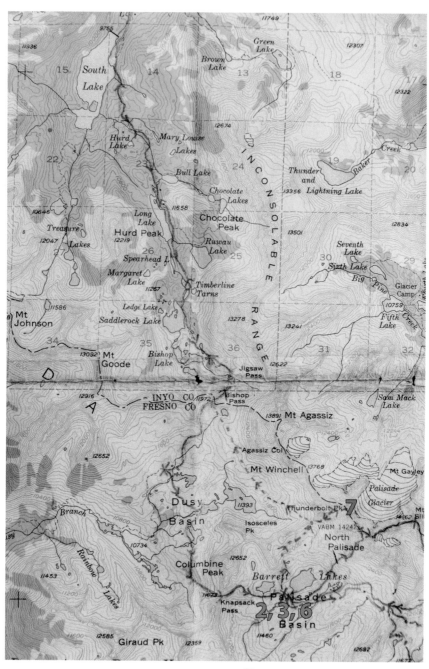

Map 8 SOD day 7 Barrett Lakes; To Thunderbolt Peak 7, To Bishop Pass & Out to South Lake

Chapter 26

MOUNT SHASTA

After a good night's sleep at the Inyo Mono Inn, we did a load of laundry and weighed ourselves. We had weighed in before we left home, and to no surprise, everyone had lost some weight. Flint went from 122 pounds to 112, Quade from 103 to 94, Cody from 72 to 63, Tyle from 56 to 49, and I went from 160 to 151 pounds. Strangely, the two smallest kids had lost the highest percentage of body weight.

We enjoyed a store-bought breakfast, then headed north on highway 395 towards Mount Shasta, our next target (see photo 237). It was August 28, 1969, day nineteen of the trip. We drove all day and into the night on a series of state highways that would eventually take us to Red Bluff, California, and Highway 5. It was close to midnight and we were a few miles from Red Bluff. We hadn't yet figured out how the calibration worked on Alan Ohlsen's fuel gauge but it turns out when the gauge read "Empty," it was. We were out of gas! Fortunately, the road we were on had a gentle downhill slope to it and we were able to coast to within about a mile of Red Bluff. No problem! The kids pushed Alan Ohlsen into a Chevron station, but I did not have a gas card for Chevron so I used a dollar's worth of change to buy gas and then drove a half mile to a Shell station where I could use my card to fill up. It turns out the luck brothers had shown up at the same time; bad luck because we had run out of gas, and good luck because we only had to push the car a mile (see photo 238).

We drove a little longer and decided to call it quits for the night. As was often the case, we found a wide spot on the side of the road, laid out our tarp and sleeping bags, and used Alan Ohlsen to shield us from oncoming traffic (see photo 239). On Friday morning, we continued north and got to the town of Mount Shasta. My sister, Dorothy, was gung-ho about what we were trying to do and had arranged for us to have interviews when we got to Mount Shasta and also at Paradise at the base of Mount Rainier.

We met a reporter, Danny Frishman, from the *Mount Shasta Herald* outside the Chamber of Commerce (see photo 240 and Appendix 5). After the interview we got a room at the Oaks Motel and had some time on our hands. We decided to scout tomorrow's route up Shasta starting at Bunny Flats Trailhead (see photos 241, 242). Mount Shasta is a lone-standing volcanic mountain. According to scientists, its last known eruption took place in 1250 A.D. With our luck it would probably explode but we took a vote and decided to climb it anyway. We ate in town and went to bed early. The next morning, Saturday, August 30, day twenty-one of our trip, we had breakfast at the Breakfast House and Tyle left his hat. So, he would have to climb Shasta without one. After nearly two weeks of messing with full packs we were glad we could do this climb with just day packs, but we did have thirteen miles to hike and 7,000 feet of elevation to gain.

At 9:30 a.m. we started hiking towards Avalanche Gulch and the Red Dyke. We found water (see photo 243) and later crossed some patches of snow containing suncups, which are bowl-shaped depressions formed when snow melts unevenly. It was our first time seeing suncups (see photo 244). Some of them were half the height of Tyle. There was a smell of sulphur from hot springs near the summit. We got to the summit at 6 p.m. and enjoyed being on top of our final California 14er (see photo 245)!

We began down (see photo 246). At 6:45 p.m., Flint began convulsing, then buckled and dropped to the ground. He was having an intense body cramp. He was lucid but had difficulty speaking. It was as though his jaw and limbs were frozen. It was scary. We tried to make him comfortable and began massaging his arms, hands, fingers and legs (see photo 247). He was probably dehydrated and needed salt. We had him drink water and when he was able to chew we gave him peanuts and beef jerky. I believe Flint's collapse was probably the result of undue stress, starting with planning the trip, setting our itinerary, gathering and organizing the equipment, packing the car, sharing driving responsibilities, the car wreck, route selection, and carrying extra climbing equipment.

After forty-five minutes, Flint's cramping subsided and he started to feel better. He was weak but able to continue down under his own power. The sun was setting and threw a dramatic shadow of Mount Shasta that rested on a layer of smoke generated by forest fires burning in northern California at that time (see photos 248-250)!

We made it back to Alan Ohlsen at 11:30 p.m. and drove into town. Unfortunately, the Breakfast House was not open at midnight; go figure. So, we couldn't get Tyle's hat until morning. I only had $4 cash left so we spent the night in our sleeping bags behind a ski-rental shop.

Photo 237 – Leaving the Inyo Mono Inn in Bishop, CA on day 19 from home August 28, 1969

Photo 238 – Finally! A gas station after pushing the car a mile to Red Bluff

Photo 239 – Roadside camp Highway 5, on our way to Mount Shasta, day 20

Photo 240 – Mt. Shasta Herald newspaper interview with Danny Frishman August 29, 1969

Photo 241 – Mount Shasta

Photo 242 – Scouting hike to check out the route on Mount Shasta

Photo 243 – Water break on Mount Shasta, day 21; August 30, 1969

Photo 244 – Getting closer

Photo 245 – Mount Shasta summit August 30, 1969

Photo 246 – Leaving the top of Mount Shasta

Photo 247 – Working on Flint's body cramp

Photo 248 – Mount Shasta's sunset shadow

Photo 249 – Colorful descent with Flint feeling better

Photo 250 – Sunset from Mount Shasta

Chapter 27

The Last One!

On Sunday morning, day twenty-two of our trip, we got Tyle's hat when the Breakfast House opened and then started driving north on Highway 5. We stopped to take a parting picture of Shasta (see photo 251) and then set our sights on Mount Rainier. On our way to Mount Rainier we were amazed at the density of the forests and the size of the gigantic trees! We stopped every hundred miles to give Alan Ohlsen his two quarts of oil (see photos 252-254). It took a full day to get out of California, drive through Oregon and cross the Columbia River into Washington. When we got to an okay pullout between White Pass and Mount Rainier National Park we quit for the night (see photo 255).

Photo 251 – Looking back (south) to Mount Shasta on day 22; August 31, 1969

Photo 252 – Oregon oil stop

Photo 253 – Oregon signpost

Photo 254 – Washington oil stop

September 1, 1969, was day twenty-three of our trip. We should have been home by now but still had one more mountain to climb. We headed for Mount Rainier National Park. As we got closer to Rainier, we were impressed with how big it looked (see photo 256)! Because of its size and many glaciers, it's known to create its own weather. But today there was not a cloud in the sky. At Paradise, we checked in at the Ranger Station to get the required permits to climb Rainier, and then went into the climbing shop and rented five pairs of crampons and four ice axes. I left my driver's license as collateral. At this point we were eighteen miles and 9,000 feet of elevation short of completing our goal of climbing all 67 of the 14ers in the contiguous forty-eight states! We had the pleasure of meeting Dee Molenaar, a renowned climber and artist at Paradise, and enjoyed talking with him about his upcoming book on Mount Rainier.

When ready, we put on our backpacks, took a photo, and headed up to Camp Muir, half way up Mount Rainier (see photos 257-259). It has a couple of stone shelters where climbers can spend the night. When we got there, they were full so we set up our tent. During the night, a relentless wind flattened our tent. None of us slept well.

216

Photo 255 – Washington roadside camp on day 23

Photo 256 – Mount Rainier

Photo 257 – At Paradise, the base of Mount Rainier (from left: Cody, Flint, Quade, Tyle, George)

Photo 258 – Paradise Trail Sign September 1, 1969

Photo 259 – Heading to Camp Muir

In the morning, we waited for the wind to die down before starting our climb, but it never did (see photo 260). We roped up and made ready to ascend (see photo 261), but never started. Instead we discussed our time-table for the day and decided to unrope and descend to Paradise to meet a reporter from *The Seattle Times* for a pre-scheduled 3 p.m. appointment.

My sister Dorothy had scheduled the interview for us ahead of time. We had misjudged big-time what it takes to climb this mountain. To keep our appointment, we would have had to start much earlier to summit and get back to Paradise. We had no way of contacting the reporter and felt obligated to keep the meeting. So, we put the tent back up, left our gear inside, and hiked down to Paradise, planning to return to our tent that evening. We waited in vain for the reporter outside the Ranger Station and after a while I found a pay phone and called *The Seattle Times* to ask what happened. They were sorry about the mixup and connected me to a reporter by the name of Dee Norton. I gave a phone interview. I was to give him a call when we were done with Rainier and he would print the article.

I rejoined the kids at Alan Ohlsen and Flint owned up to the fact that he was not feeling good. Actually, he couldn't even walk. We talked about the options and decided he would spend the night in the car. So we went up to Camp Muir without him (see photo 262). Tomorrow we would attempt to summit Mount Rainier and return to Paradise. Once at Camp Muir we cooked dinner and went to bed. We knew we would have to get up in a few hours and didn't get much sleep. I had some minor anxiety about climbing on the upper slopes of Mount Rainier because there were crevasses to navigate and none of us had used an ice axe on a glacier before. Flint would normally lead our roped team up the mountain but he was back at the car, so Quade would have to lead us.

Photo 260 – Wind blew our tent down last night at Camp Muir, morning of day 24

Photo 261 – Pit stop for Tyle at Camp Muir

Photo 262 – Going back to Camp Muir after phone interview with the Seattle Times, without Flint

At 4 a.m. on September 3, 1969, day twenty-five of our trip, we had a light breakfast inside the tent and prepared for our summit attempt. It was windy again, but we didn't let that stop us because we had this last mountain to climb. We put on our crampons, tied into our goldline rope as one team, and started off, each with an ice axe. Soon after leaving, our route dropped out of the wind. We later learned that it is nearly always windy at Camp Muir because of where it is situated. We saw the sunrise over Little Tahoma Peak and were in awe of the beauty around us (see photo 263). We chose to climb the Disappointment Cleaver route. The fact that we were roped together resulted in a heightened awareness of each other and a focus on our climbing. We did a good job of pacing and spacing ourselves as a team of four so the rope did not yank anyone forward or gather at anyone's feet (see photos 264-266).

We reached the lip of the summit crater and then headed to the highest point, Columbia Crest. Once on top I had strong feelings about what was taking place. Rainier was the final 14er in our quest to climb all 67 in the contiguous forty-eight states. It was the culmination of a minimum of four years' effort by us that was coming to an end. Along this journey, there had always been another mountain for me to climb, another challenge to meet in life's struggles, but this was the last one. I was happy at our success, and I was sad at the same time that this chapter was almost over. Also, Flint wasn't here and I felt an emptiness about that. I wanted us all to finish this journey together. I wondered how he would handle this.

It was 1 p.m. when we summited. We left at 1:45 p.m. It was still quite windy (see photo 267) when we started to head down (see photos 268, 269). We got to Camp Muir at 4:45 p.m. and took down the tent. We packed up and also had Flint's stuff to deal with. Quade carried some of it and Cody carried Flint's pack. Tyle carried Cody's pack and I carried Tyle's pack plus my own (see photo 270). We headed down at 6:15 p.m. On our way down we passed through a layer of clouds at around 8,000 feet that hindered visibility, but we knew how to get to Paradise because we had just been there yesterday (see photos 271, 272). It was 9:30 p.m. when we got to Flint at Paradise. He was happy to see us and was feeling better, but I am sure that his decision to remain at Paradise was weighing on him. The climbing shop was closed and so was the Ranger Station, so we put the ice axes and crampons in the after-hours return box along with a note. The note instructed, "To Whom It May Concern," to please mail my driver's license to me at my home address in Denver. We left money for postage. The boys repacked the car for the drive back to Denver and I used a pay phone to call *The Seattle Times* to confirm with Dee Norton that we had made the summit (see Appendix 6). It was about 10 p.m. when we started home.

Photo 263 – Little Tahoma Peak at sunrise on day 25; September 3, 1969

Photo 264 – Line of climbers ascending Mount Rainier

Photo 265 – On the Disappointment Cleaver route

Photo 266 – Working our way through suncups

Photo 267 – On the summit of Mount Rainier, our 67th 14er, minus Flint, September 3, 1969

Photo 268 – Heading back down the Disappointment Cleaver route

Photo 269 – Aiming for Camp Muir in the saddle

Photo 270 – Packed up and ready to leave Camp Muir

Photo 271 – Low clouds ahead

Photo 272 – We're in those low clouds

It took us two days to drive back to Denver, making regular stops to feed oil to Alan Ohlsen (see photo 273). We got home really late on Friday night, September 5th. The trip had taken twenty-seven days. We unloaded the car on Saturday (see photo 274), and weighed in. I weighed 151 pounds, Flint 115 pounds, Quade 100 pounds, Cody 70 pounds and Tyle weighed 56 pounds. On Monday I took Alan Ohlsen to Lawrence Berridge Auto for a checkup. Lawrence gave it a once-over and was surprised we made it back at all. We had driven over 3,000 miles in Alan Ohlsen and Lawrence told us that only three of the six cylinders were working. He said, "You must have a lucky rock in your pocket." The boys missed the first week of school but it was an okay trade-off. What they will have gained from this adventure will last a lifetime.

"Life is a climb and the route taken determines the rewards."
G. NASH SMITH

Photo 273 – Idaho oil stop on day 26; September 4, 1969

Photo 274 – Back home only 4 days behind schedule! Unloading Alan Ohlsen the next day,
September 6, 1969. Yee haaw, good job boys!

Chapter 28

DISAPPOINTMENT HAD A PURPOSE

It turns out there was a major hidden benefit resulting from Flint not climbing Rainier with us, but it would be the next year before we would learn what that was. Flint was disappointed and knew he wanted to climb Rainier as soon as he could, and did so on June 11, 1970, as a student in a Rainier Mountaineering Incorporated (RMI) course (see photos 275, 276). In addition to his joining us in having climbed them all he benefitted from that experience in other ways. He returned home with more skills pertaining to snow and ice and his RMI experience flamed his growing interest in teaching other kids about the mountains. "Way to go, Flint."

"Live your life so as to be a credit to your family."
G. NASH SMITH

Flint went to college at Western State in Gunnison from September 1970 through June 1974. He helped start a climbing club and a mountain rescue team that did a lot of rock climbing up Taylor Canyon. He discovered his climbing skills were unique compared to the others. He had a higher comfort level on steep rock than most. In April of 1971, during his freshman year, he applied for and was offered a job with the Ashcrofters Mountaineering School, a climbing school in Aspen under the direction of Dave Farney, who was impressed that Flint had climbed all of the 14ers in the contiguous forty-eight states. But hold on! When Henry Barber, a well-known rock climber, became available to go back to work for the Ashcrofters, Farney rescinded his offer to Flint. To heck with that....

Naturally, Flint was disappointed and deflated. Flint and I had a long talk about it. No problem. And here's where Flint's disappointments turned into a major hidden benefit. "The Climbing Smiths School of Mountaineering," (CSSM) was born. We would develop our own outdoor program starting this summer with Flint as the lead instructor. The motto for our school was, "Not if, but how." It would be a family undertaking.

Quade, Cody and Tyle would also be instructors. Quade participated in a National Outdoor Leadership School (NOLS) course in Wyoming in June, before we conducted our very first session in July 1971. We operated in the summers from 1971-1978 with week-long sessions for boys aged 12-18. We taught seven-day mountaineering and life-skills courses in the Maroon Bells Snowmass Wilderness area. When one parent asked why we chose an area so rugged and dangerous, I replied that he had answered his own question. I said, "If you can learn to climb there, you can climb anywhere."

In the summer of 1974 I felt we were ready for another adventure and we decided as a family to attempt to climb all 68 acknowledged 14ers in the contiguous forty-eight states in one continuous trip (the official number of 14ers had increased by one with the addition of Ellingwood Point). We set out to go as fast as we could as a self-supported team using "safe" means. This meant we did not skip sleep, or start a climb at night. Also, we took rest days. As it turns out, we climbed all 68 14ers in forty-eight days. The stories of that undertaking may be told at another time (see photo 277).

Photo 275 – Flint's RMI group climbing Mount Rainier in 1970

Photo 276 – Flint on the summit of Mount Rainier June 11, 1970

Photo 277 – The Climbing Smiths (from left: Quade, George, Flint, Tyle, Cody) on the summit of Mount Rainier, after climbing all 68 14ers in 48 days from July 4, 1974 through August 20, 1974

Chapter 29

REFLECTIONS

Just start walking and see how far you can go. That was my strategy. That's what I did when I began climbing. It worked until Warren and I got on North Maroon. That turned out to be too big of a jump from what we had done prior. It was far more difficult than the nine peaks that I had climbed before that. I was climbing over my head and wasn't prepared. We were lucky to get down safely. I knew not to do that with the boys. When we began climbing as a family, we used a stairstep approach starting with easy peaks and then intermediate peaks, working our way up to the more difficult 14ers. I'm really proud of our climbing all the 14ers without anyone getting hurt. There were some close calls, but we had good luck as well, and were able to make it on our own. None of us had prior training when we started. Nobody went to anyone's class. We liked to figure out our own route. We weren't in charge on just two of our climbs. Bill Arnold led us on the Crestones and the Maroon Bells. We developed our own set of hiker/climber guidelines that helped us and we taught them in our mountaineering school. They are listed in Appendix 7.

My sisters were 10 years and 7 years older than me and because of that age spread we didn't share a lot of time together. I just knew I had two older sisters. With my own sons there is a 7-year difference but because of our climbing together and having the chance to save each other's life there is no age difference. For me, the best thing to come out of our family climbing is that Flint, Quade, Cody, Tyle and I are a team.

SUNSET

Me? I prefer a sunset. I live to enjoy another sunset;
But not a city sunset.

True, a sunset signals the death of a day;
The past just gained another day,
But what a day!

The struggle and strain to reach a summit
Repays many fold when you get to the top;
The ultimate is… a sunset summit.

THANKS LORD

Thanks Lord, for Another Day.

Happy New Day sounds better to me
Than the traditional "Happy New Year";
'Cause one sun at a time is all that we get,
Tomorrow's sun has yet to appear.

The older one gets the faster time passes,
And the slower the footsteps occur;
It won't last forever, one day life will end,
And on that slice of wisdom we concur.

Today was a good day in spite of some challenges,
But with caution I made it thru;
And if tomorrow should happen and I see the sun,
My life will begin anew.
AMEN!

"Life's journey: Do I have any regrets? Yes, but I have yet to meet anyone I would want to trade places with."

G. NASH SMITH

Over and out

Appendix 1

George in a Denver Post article by Frank Haraway, 1945

The above *Denver Post* article written by Frank Haraway, dated May 13, 1945, states:

"East's George Smith
is called 'Pete Gray'
of Prep Ball Loop"

   One of the most amazing stories ever to come out of the Denver prep league—and one that should be a great inspiration to disabled war veterans—is that of George Smith, East high outfielder, who plays brilliant baseball for the Angels despite a hand minus all but one finger that makes him a one-armed player for all practical purposes.

Smith stole the show Saturday even though his East Angels lost to North, 3-2. All he did was step up to the plate with his one good arm, bang a hot line double to right field, get one other hit off the league's ace pitcher, Virgil Jester, and race into right center for a breath-taking circus catch of a low line drive, turning a complete somersault after nabbing the flying horsehide. He also made one other catch that was considerably above the average. The rest of his play was flawless throughout. Last week he smacked a triple.

The Pete Gray* of the prep loop, as he is called by unbelieving fans who have seen him in action, lost a portion of his right arm in a freak mishap a few days before his fourth birthday back on May 9, 1932.

The arm was so severely damaged most of the hand had to be amputated and the entire lower extremity of the arm withered after it was nearly torn off when a neighbor's car, backing out of a garage, caught it between the car door and a post dividing a two-car garage. But the sorrel-topped youngster, whose older brothers, Tupper and Keene, made basketball history at East high, refused to let this tragic mishap—a handicap that would keep all but the hardiest of youngsters from even thinking about athletics—discourage him.

Young George, with his older brothers ever an inspiration to him, played right along with them—in fact he plays more sports than they do. George was one of the outstanding football players in the Young America league playing for the Denver Athletic club as a back and an end. In basketball he was good enough to win a letter last winter at East—is a great shot with his left hand. In addition to baseball, football and basketball he has even boxed and is a standout swimmer.

George, who is 5 feet 10 inches tall and weighs 145 pounds and will be 17 years old June 1, is also a leader among boys, is an Eagle Boy Scout and assistant scoutmaster of Troop 1, and is probably the most popular boy in East high school today. As a student he has a B average and is just a shade below the grades needed to qualify him as a candidate for head boy which his friends say he could win hands down.

Most important, he is extremely modest, and makes light of his athletic prowess and the handicap he has overcome.

He is a junior at East and after graduation expects to go to an agricultural college to prepare for the cattle business. If this plan doesn't materialize, George will attend Colorado University, where his older brothers, Tupper and Keene, starred on the cage court last winter.'

*Following is a summary of an article about Pete Gray by Dave Garcia in the Denver Post July 23, 2001: Pete Gray was a one-armed outfielder who played for the St. Louis Browns in 1945. While this was the only year he played in the big leagues, he played several years in the minor leagues. He got 51 hits and batted .218 in 77 games. Pete had six doubles and two triples in 234 at-bats. Gray had a left arm but not a right arm due to a boyhood accident that caused his right arm to be lost above the elbow. In the article, Dave Garcia states, "It was absolutely amazing how he would catch a flyball, flip the ball in the air, tuck his glove under his little, short arm and throw."

Ribbon Winner

Colorado's Chinchilla Champ Scorns Coats

"Fudge," Colorado's only blue-ribbon-winner at the National Chinchilla show Friday through Sunday at Minneapolis, Minn., was home Wednesday, modestly wriggling her nose over the achievement.

Fudge, who headquarters at the Kamer-Nash Chinchilla ranch, 743 St. Paul St., also took two red ribbons. All ribbons attested her superiority as a "medium pale," young (6 months) chinchilla.

NO COAT FOR HER

As a result she rated among the top 12 animals out of 286 entered in the national show.

As a valuable breeding animal, "Fudge" will perpetuate her breed instead of going into a coat at any time in the near future.

Pelts from 26 of her less-fortunate companions at the Kamer-Nash ranch are expected to be sold at the first chinchilla fur auction this summer in New York.

The auction will precede the first production of the gray, angora-soft chinchilla fur coats for public sale. However, the first coats probably will be priced between $50,000 and $75,000, George Nash Smith, co-partner with Warren Kamer Pulis in the Kamer-Nash ranch, estimated.

Valuable at almost any level, a pair of fine breeding chinchilla animals, like "Fudge," are worth from $1,200 to $1,500.

Denver Post Photo.
Here are George Nash Smith of Denver and Fudge, who was the only blue ribbon winner from Colorado at the National Chinchilla show.

George and "Fudge," a prize-winning chinchilla, 1951

Appendix 2

INDEXED   COMPARED.   INDEXED

121423
No.

121424
No.

Location Certificate

Location Certificate

On the....Palebutt No. 1............Lode

On the....Palebutt No. 2............Lode

Mining Claim of...Warren K. Pulis &....

Mining Claim of...Warren K. Pulis &....

...George N. Smith..................

George N. Smith

in....Harrington............. Mining

in....Harrington............. Mining

District,....Park............County,
State of Colorado.

District,....Park............County,
State of Colorado.

STATE OF COLORADO, } ss.

STATE OF COLORADO, } ss.

County of....Park............

Counte of....Park............

I hereby certify that this Location Certificate was filed for record in my office at ..3:30..o'clock P M., ...July 20, 19..54.., and is duly recorded in Book..43 at Page....203......

I hereby certify that this Location Certificate was filed for record in my office at ..3:31..o'clock P M., ...July 20, 19..54.., and is duly recorded in Book..43 at Page....204......

Marjorie M. Richardson
-----RECORDER

Marjorie M. Richardson
-----RECORDER

By....Lois Lewis....
-----DEPUTY

By....Lois Lewis....
-----DEPUTY

Fees, $ 1.40 Pd

Fees, $ 1.40 Pd

WHEN RECORDED RETURN TO

WHEN RECORDED RETURN TO

Warren K. Pulis

OUT WEST PRTG. & STATY. CO., COLORADO SPRINGS M7358

OUT WEST PRTG. & STATY. CO., COLORADO SPRINGS M7358

Two Mining Claims, July 20, 1954

Appendix 3

August 22, 1968   The Aspen Times   Page 1-B

THE ASPEN TIMES

Section B

Eight-year old Tyle Smith of Denver (center) did in the Aspen area last month what probably no other boy of his age has ever done. He completed the ascent of all 53 of Colorado's 14,000-ft. peaks. Tyle did the feat by topping 14,077-ft. Snowmass Mountain the Snowmass-Maroon Bells Wilderness Area on July 15. He, his three older brothers and father were photographed by a member of the Ashcrofters Mountaineering School at 9:30 AM just under the summit. The family calls itself the Outpost Mountaineering Club. Members are (l. to r. above), Cody, 11; club father George; Tyle; Flint, 16; and Quade, 12. Earlier the club tackled North and South Maroon Bells. It took two hours to cross between the two peaks. Fifteen boys were in the Ashcrofters' party. They were led by guides Jim Ward, Bill Harper and Greg Simmons.

The Aspen Times article (from left: Cody, George, Tyle, Flint, Quade), July 1968

238

Appendix 4

A father who always hated to give up taught his four sons the lessons of life

The saga of

Breaking through the clouds, the four sons of George Smith near the summit of 14,265-foot Castle Peak in the Maroon Bells-Snowmass Wilderness south of Aspen.

The Smiths at ease on top of Mt. Harvard.

10   Oct. 13, 1968 • EMPIRE MAGAZINE

The Denver Post's Empire Magazine: "The Saga of the Climbing Smiths," by Cal Queal, October 13, 1968 (page 1 of 5 pages)

on the rugged trails to Colorado's high peaks

the climbing Smiths By CAL QUEAL

ON A sunny day last July George Smith and his four sons climbed 14,092 - foot Snowmass Peak in the Maroon Bells-Snowmass Wilderness west of Aspen. Of little consequence itself, the fact becomes interesting when one learns Smith has only one good arm and that his youngest son, Tyle, was then a mere 8 years old.

The truly remarkable thing is that Snowmass was the very last on the list of Colorado's 53 famous "Fourteeners" (peaks over 14,000 feet) Smith and his sons have conquered. And that isn't the whole story, either.

The way it happened, the adventure it produced and the rationale behind it all amount to something more than the usual success story. With only the slightest bit of literary license one could call it the Saga of the Climbing Smiths.

George Nash Smith is 40, and his businesses are the Old West Real Estate Co. and square dance calling. On a five-acre plot just east of Denver he has a large home with an exterior finished in dark-stained, rough-texture wood that gives it an alpine look, and a large square dance "barn" of the same appearance.

The spacious barn provided the setting for an interview and a showing of some of the hundreds of color slides Smith has taken while climbing and hiking in the Colorado Rockies. Each picture that flashed on the screen recalled a special occasion to Smith, and his running commentary reflected much about his character and credo. It added up to a good time and place for finding out what makes George Smith tick, or, more accurately, hum.

The motivations of any particular man for climbing mountains are likely to be very personal and therefore obscure. George Smith was able to make his sons feel them almost as strongly as he did. It follows that the motivations are quite special.

Freckled, red-haired Tyle A, now 9, is the youngest in history to have climbed all of Colorado's above-14,000 peaks. The oldest boy, Flint K, is only 15. In the middle are Quade B, 12, and Cody J, 11. People often comment that the boys'

first names, and single-letter middle names are quite distinctive—a fact that pleases their father. Having been one of thousands of George Smiths, he was determined his sons would have no such identification problems.

Like most mountain men Smith is essentially quiet and reserved. Anyone who talks to him at length, however, especially about mountaineering, begins to feel the intensity of purpose that burns behind his cool, gray-blue eyes. At 5 feet 10 and 150 pounds he is not a big man, but solid, and one senses that he's mentally tough. The reasons for that may go back to 1932, when his right arm was mangled in an automobile accident.

The arm is withered and crooked. Instead of a hand at the end there is a stump with two stiff fingers. Yet Smith used it to good effect when he was a standout on the baseball team at East High School, where he also lettered in basketball. He played in the Young America Football League, and at Colorado State University was active in intramural sports.

Somehow he makes the same bad arm do the job in the life and death business of mountain climbing. It seems inappropriate to refer to him as "handicapped" and nobody does. Perhaps the first to ignore the fact of the bad arm were his two older brothers.

"We used to play games, wrestle and that sort of thing, and they never let me feel sorry for myself," Smith recalls. "I didn't get any special breaks from them, and I guess I found out I didn't really need or want special breaks. You could say I wanted to do it myself."

George Smith has been doing things for himself determinedly, even since. Mountaineering provided a demanding proving grounds for the development of his credo.

A person aspiring to climb mountains usually joins a club or hires an instructor. Smith did neither. Starting while a student at CSU, he climbed on weekends with a friend, Warren Pulis, now a resident of Vail. Smith had been an Eagle Scout, so he knew something about knots, but that was about it. He and Pulis learned climbing techniques, the use of ropes, carabiners, pitons and other gear simply by doing.

"I don't expect everyone to understand this," says Smith, "but I didn't want someone to lead me up those mountains. I didn't want to be told how or shown how. I had to do it my way."

Many experienced climbers deplore such attitudes on the grounds that inexperience and trouble go hand in hand when it comes to climbing. There are many people who should climb only after a full course of instruction, and others who should never climb at all. Then there are people like George Smith. With determination, an understanding of basic principles of physics, and uncommonly good c o m m o n sense, he was able to teach himself.

When he had n e a r l y finished climbing the 53 peaks, Smith bought some books on mountaineering. In such matters as climbing technique and the use of equipment, he found the experts confirming what he'd learned through experience.

On each of the state's higher peaks is a register where climbers write in their names and club identifications. Often the club name is abbreviated — the last two letters most commonly b e i n g MC, for mountain club. Smith had no club affiliation, but wanted to w r i t e in something besides his own name. He started putting down "OMC".

"That was for 'Own Mountain Club'," says Smith, laughing a little at himself. "Later we formed a family club, with shoulder patches and all, and called it the Outpost Mountain Club. So we're still 'OMC'."

Smith's f i r s t Fourteener was Longs Peak (14,256 feet), which he climbed with Pulis in 1948. Another cf the early ones with Pulis was La Plata Peak (14,336 feet) in the Sawatch Range, just south of Independence Pass, where Smith f i r s t began to form a kind of philosophy about mountain climbing and life.

"When we started out, the peak looked impossibly high and difficult," says Smith. "Still we decided to give it a try, and as we moved ahead the peak just seemed to flatten out. We were on top almost before we knew it.

"Life is like that, you know. When something looks tough, take the first step, then the next. It won't be long before the last step to the top—over the problem."

In August of 1951 George married

Marilou Milano of Denver, and the couple's honeymoon took them, after a trip to Wyoming's Tetons, to the top of Mt. Democrat (14,148 feet), in the Mosquito Range, northwest of Fairplay. Smith had spotted an old bellows in an ice bank on the mountain that spring, and August seemed like a good time to pick it up and give his bride some mountain climbing experience.

The climb proved exceedingly tough for her. George finally had to carry most of the gear and the 56-pound bellows as well.

To ease the burden, he found a steep slope relatively free of rocks and tried rolling one of the packs. As both of them watched helplessly, the pack gained momentum quickly, bounding high in the air, and finally split wide open, scattering the contents over the mountainside.

Earlier, Mrs. Smith had accidentally broken her glasses. The rough going had produced several rents in her blue jeans and she was bleeding from various lacerations when they finally got back to Fairplay. It was, in short, a horrible experience for the newlyweds.

"I didn't start her out very well," says Smith ruefully.

"There was almost an annulment," says Mrs. Smith, but she can laugh now at something which, when it happened, wasn't the least bit funny.

Game enough, she climbed several more times with her husband, and each time there was some special kind of trouble. After climbing five of the Fourteeners Mrs. Smith gave up. She still enjoys the mountains, but is content to let the men of the family tackle the high peaks.

Smith climbed 15 Fourteeners in 1956, bringing his total to 29. That's when he started thinking about getting all 53, but his fast-growing family forced a postponement. Flint was three that year, and Quade was born. A year later came Cody, and less than three years after that, Tyle.

The boys got into the act in 1962, when Flint and Quade, then 10 and 6 years, respectively, climbed Mt. Sherman (14,036 feet). Cody started in 1964 at age 7 on Mt. Democrat, where his mother had her ill-fated initiation. Tyle started on Mt. Sherman in 1966 at the age of 6.

"We'd grab another peak or two when we could find a free weekend,"

continued

Color photography by George Smith

The Denver Post's Empire Magazine: "The Saga of the Climbing Smiths," by Cal Queal,
October 13, 1968 (page 2 of 5 pages)

The Smith sons and a friend begin the long walk to the top of 14,197-foot Mt. Belford in the Sawatch Mountains south of Leadville.

SMITH SAGA continued

says Smith. "Nobody had to go. I'd just say 'Who wants to climb' and we'd go from there. Flint didn't like it at first but he eventually caught fire.

"There were times when I was probably a little too tough, Tyle complained about not feeling well once and yet I talked him into climbing. We got up Mt. Antero (14,269 feet) and were going to get another one when it became obvious he was really sick. We headed for home; the doctor took a look and said he had German measles."

Friends sometimes wonder if Smith pushes his sons too hard.

"I demand a lot from them," says Smith. "But I'm always fair and consistent. They don't get much sympathy from me but they get all the time I can spare and a lot of what I think is good advice. I got them started on the mountains, but they made the decisions to stay with it."

Heading for the summits, the Smiths have often encountered climbers who turned back because of weather or other difficulties. Weather has never stopped the Smiths. Rain hardly slows them down, and they have conquered

some of the peaks in driving snow-storms.

"Bad weather makes the climb tougher, of course," says Smith. "But I want the boys to learn that you don't quit just because things get tough. When they get tired I try to talk them into slowing down instead of stopping. Once you get going good and you stop, your legs stiffen up and it's hard to get moving again."

The three older boys made three climbing trips in 1964 and six in 1965. Activity picked up in 1966, when Tyle joined the group, and 19 trips were made. Smith recalls the day Tyle made his first climb.

"We'd all been talking it up for him," he says. "It was a great moment when we pulled the car up to the jumping off place for Mt. Sherman, and we were all wanting Tyle to get off to a good start."

Young Tyle promptly shattered their illusions by falling down a small precipice when he got out of the car. He pulled himself together, however, and the five Smiths started up the trail. Tyle went about 100 yards, sat down and to everyone's consternation announced that he was too tired to go further. Smith laughs as he recalls the day:

"I sat down with Tyle and told

him that it wasn't going to be easy, but that he really could do it if he just kept putting one foot ahead of the other. He finally got going good, and in no time at all he was on top of Mt. Sherman. He's been going as hard as any of us ever since."

In 1967 the Smiths made 29 trips, and their tally of Fourteeners stood at 37 by the end of the season. Late last May, when some of the snow had started to melt above timberline, they climbed Mt. Massive (14,421 feet), near Leadville, then went south into the Sawatch Range where they got Mount Princeton (14,197 feet) and Huron Peak (14,005 feet). A weekend in the Lake City area got them San Luis Peak (14,014 feet) and then it was back to the Collegiate Peaks again for Mount Harvard (14,420 feet).

On one trip north of Fort Garland they added Mt. Lindsey (14,125 feet), Blanca Peak (14,317 feet) and Little Bear Peak (14,037 feet). Things were going on schedule, with no problems. Then the Smiths ran into trouble on Capitol Peak, June 29.

The climb up went well, even on the treacherous knife edge ridge leading to the summit of the 14,130-foot peak. On the summit at about 6 p.m., they still had two hours of good light, and headed back down

the ridge. Part way across there was a choice of taking a difficult part of the ridge or going below into the snow. The lower route was the logical choice, but in this particular case it brought trouble.

There was a steep snowfield to cross and the surface, which had been soft earlier, had turned into an icy crust. The Smiths got out the ropes, and Flint made it across the field where he anchored one end of the 150-foot rope. Smith held the other while Cody went across, holding on to the rope. Then it was Tyle's turn.

In the middle of the snowfield, Tyle lost his footing, sliding about 10 feet before the rope stopped him. He was hanging on with his hands, on a 60-degree slope, with 500 feet of ice below him ending in a mass of jagged rocks. It was a heartstopper for everyone.

"I knew he'd be all right if he could get his arms over the rope," says Smith. "I had to anchor the end, so I sent Quade after him. We finally got everyone across, but by now it was dark and the flashlight had given out."

The Smiths found a small niche in the rock, partly sheltered from the wind, and curled up for the night. The temperature dropped well below

continued

The Denver Post's Empire Magazine: "The Saga of the Climbing Smiths," by Cal Queal, October 13, 1968 (page 3 of 5 pages)

SMITH SAGA *continued*

low freezing, and everyone had slightly frost-bitten toes in the morning, but they made it out and down without further incident.

Is Smith conscious of the danger to which he exposes his sons?

"Of course we think about the danger," says Smith, "but we think about it all the time. It never takes us by surprise. I tell the boys 'you only get one chance' and 'you can only make one mistake', and they know it's true. With their mountain experience, when I tell them they can only make one bad mistake while riding their bikes—turning in front of a car, for instance—it really sinks in."

Only George has been badly injured during the five years the Smith family has been climbing the Fourteeners. At the end of a slide down a snowfield, Smith crashed into a pile of rocks and bruised his tailbone. It hardly slowed him down on his alpine conquest. At various times he has climbed with a sprained ankle, a fractured knee cap and when weak from influenza.

Tyle once fell forward while hiking on Pike's Peak and cut his lip. His father's comment was simply: "He learned not to walk with his hands in his pockets."

Among mountaineers there is wide disagreement over which Colorado peaks are more difficult. Each climb, in fact, may be more or less difficult depending on the route taken, the weather, or simply conditions of the moment—a falling rock, a slab of ice, the time of day that forces a faster but more difficult route.

The Colorado Mountain Club classifies peaks in such a way that anyone who follows their rating system will be prepared for most of the possible problems. The club lists 10 as being "difficult, with rope" (Crestone Peak, Crestone Needle, Capitol Peak, North Maroon Peak, Maroon Peak, Pyramid Peak, Wetterhorn Peak, Wilson Peak, Mt. Wilson, and El Diente). Smith says a climber who takes the right route wouldn't need a rope on any of them.

He and his sons used a rope only four times in the course of climbing the 53 Fourteeners. They roped up between Crestone Peak and Crestone Needle and between North Maroon and Maroon Peaks, although any one of the four could be climbed individually without rope, according to Smith. Because of special circumstances they used ropes going up Pyramid Peak (14,018 feet) and coming down Capitol Peak.

Smith says that of the 30 mountains classified as moderately difficult by the club, only about a half dozen involve "exposure"—precarious places where a slip would mean a bad fall. Under these circumstances, many climbers rope up. At least 10 peaks are "walk-ups," according to Smith.

Predictably, the kids are excellent climbers. Flint, who at first cared little for climbing, is the best of the group on technical matters. Quade and Cody often lead—a job usually reserved in a group only for the best climbers. The fastest climber in the group is Tyle, who often confounds experienced climbers with his speed and dexterity.

"I saw those kids climbing Mt. Eolus in the San Juans this summer," says Larry Fidler of the Colorado Mountain Club. "I was amazed to see them move so fast—they're great."

Their very smallness gives the younger boys an advantage over adults. With a different perspective in relation to the rock, they can see hand and footholds larger people would pass up. And once they see them, their smaller hands and feet can grip them more easily.

The Smiths often go up their mountains non-stop. Smith has a theory that it takes time to get one's system working at top efficiency again after a rest stop. "Keep 'em churning," is his advice to the boys.

When they want to stop, he asks them to first try slowing down, and it usually is enough.

"Sometimes we go so slow we're practically standing still," says Smith.

Many of the Fourteeners can be climbed in a day. On others an overnight camp is necessary, and the boys are quite accustomed to carrying heavy packs. Despite his small size (4 feet 2, 49 pounds) Tyle, carries an old U.S. Army rucksack. The metal frame hangs down below his

CONTINUED

Like all climbers, the Smiths move slowly over the "knife edge" approaching 14,130-foot Capitol Peak.

The Denver Post's Empire Magazine: "The Saga of the Climbing Smiths," by Cal Queal,
October 13, 1968 (page 4 of 5 pages)

SMITH SAGA *continued*

hips, giving him an unduly bulky look, but doesn't slow him down.

The Smith climbing party often has a sixth member—Mocha, a nine-year-old female shepherd dog. She loves the mountains, is cool in tight situations, and carries the "dog rope"—70 feet of small nylon line in a coil around her neck and front leg. Mocha has climbed 30 of the Fourteeners, and Smith says he thinks she could do 45 of them without undue difficulty.

A climbing weekend that would seem impossibly rigorous to most people is routine for the Smiths. The schedule for a recent outing in southwestern Colorado isn't untypical.

Smith and the boys left Denver in the family station wagon Wednesday, July 3, reaching Durango at 10 p.m. After spending the night camped in a roadside park, they boarded the famous Rio Grande narrow gauge train to Silverton Thursday morning.

They left the train at the Needleton stop south of Silverton at 11:15 a.m., shouldered their packs and started the seven-mile trip to Chicago Basin—a popular climbers' rendezvous and jumping off point for three Fourteeners. Passing a number of hikers along the trail, they gained 3,000 feet in elevation and were in the basin after only three hours of hiking.

Most campers would have camped for the night and started climbing the next day. The Smiths paused only long enough to get some weight out of their packs then scrambled to the top of Mt. Eolus (14,084 feet). They were back in camp at 9 p.m.

They climbed again the next day, despite a three-hour snowstorm that made the upper slopes treacherous. When they got back to camp at 5 p.m. Friday they had added Windom and Sunlight peaks to their list.

Saturday was more or less leisurely occupied hiking seven miles back down to Needleton, boarding the train, and spending a few hours in Silverton. The train took them back to Durango, where the Smiths piled into the station wagon again at 6 p.m. and headed for the Silver Pick Mine, south of Placerville.

They arrived at their campsite at 10:30 p.m., tackled 14,159-foot El Diente in a snowstorm early Sunday morning, got back down at 10 p.m., drove all night and reached Denver the next morning at 6:30.

Expeditions like these are filled with small crises and unexpected difficulties. Less determined climbers could never get through such a trip.

"It's so easy to find reasons to quit," says Smith. "Some people never accomplish much in their lifetimes because of that. If you can ignore the reasons for quitting, you probably will decide later they weren't very good reasons, anyway.

Orin A. Sealy

Ready to move, George Smith looks over his crew of climbers, (left to right) Quade, Cody, Tyle, Mocha (the dog) and Flint.

"I can remember a few times when I swore I'd never go up another mountain if I could just get off the one I was on," he continues. "But after I got down, and the tough part was just a memory, it wasn't long before I was ready to go again."

The Smith saga came to a climax July 15 on 14,092-foot Snowmass Peak. They had all climbed treacherous North Maroon (14,014 feet) and Maroon (14,156 feet) peaks the day before, and their four-year project was near an end.

They left the campground at the end of the road on Snowmass Creek about noon and made the nine-mile hike into Snowmass Lake in leisurely fashion, playing at the creek crossings, enjoying the scenery.

"It was quite a bit different from the other climbs," Smith recalls. "It was great to realize we were almost through, but in a way we were all a little sorry to see it end."

They camped that night at the lake, and around the light of the fire talked about the "other 52." In the course of reminiscing, each Smith agreed he'd do it all over again.

"I'll remember a long time something Flint said that night," says Smith. "He said that after finding a way to the top of all those peaks he thought he'd be able to discover a lot of handholds and footholds in the mountain of life—places he might not find if he didn't really try hard."

They started up Snowmass at 7:15 the next morning, and arrived on top at 11:15. The weather was perfect.

"We goofed around on top for about an hour, taking pictures and enjoying the view," says Smith. "We could see the Maroon Bells off to the south, Capitol Peak, where we'd had so much trouble, on the north, and that beautiful green valley down below.

"On the way back, we stopped to talk to another group of climbers. They were amazed to hear we'd just climbed the last of the Fourteeners. One of the climbers said he was proud to shake our hands, and he really meant it. It made us all feel good."

Late in the long Fourteener conquest, incidents like this made Smith wonder just how other people would view their accomplishment.

"I'd never wanted to talk much about it before," he says. "But near the end I had a change of mind. Suddenly I didn't want to keep it to myself any longer. Now that it's all over I want everyone to know."

The Smiths only recently joined the Colorado Mountain Club. Typically, George felt like becoming a member only after he'd proven himself as a mountaineer—alone. The five Smiths are among about 100 people who have climbed all 53 of Colorado's high peaks.

Since he started in 1948, Smith has made 110 climbs of over-14,000 peaks. He "lost" Grizzly Peak in 1963 and Stewart Peak in 1966 when new surveys placed these two mountains short of 14,000 feet. With the Colorado challenge gone, Smith is considering the remaining above-14,000 peaks in the contiguous 48 states. There are 15 in California and one in Washington. Smith thinks they could get them all in a month or less.

Friends have asked George Smith just how much of the determination the boys demonstrated on the peaks they will be able to transfer to the jobs and problems later in life.

"Sure, the problems will be different than those they faced on the peaks," he says. "But when they have a choice of taking the next step or giving up, when they're down and need to bounce back, I think all this will come back and hit them right in the seat of the pants.

"They're not going to be afraid to try, and they're sure not going to quit without a battle. That's what they learned on those mountains. I'll bet they never forget it."

+ + +

The Denver Post's Empire Magazine: "The Saga of the Climbing Smiths," by Cal Queal,

October 13, 1968 (page 5 of 5 pages)

Appendix 5

Mount Shasta Herald article (from left: Flint, Quade, Cody, Tyle, and George) 1969

Photo caption: "The Climbing Smiths of Denver, Colo., have scaled all of the peaks in the continental United States over 14,000 feet with the exception of Mt. Shasta and Rainier. They were in town last week to climb Shasta on Saturday and then climb Rainier to complete their record. They are shown above with two small packs they carry with them. In the party are Flint, 17; Quade, 13; Cody, 12; Tyle, 10; and George, their father."

Colorado Mountaineers
"Climbing Smiths" near goal with Shasta climb

With their ascent of Mt. Shasta last Saturday the Smith family, of Denver Colo., have only Mt. Rainier left to climb to have conquered all the peaks in the continental United States over 14,000 feet.

The Smith men – Mrs. Smith stayed at home – left Colorado with the aim of climbing the fourteen remaining peaks they needed to conquer for their goal. Since that time they have climbed twelve and as of last Friday had only Mt. Shasta and Rainier remaining.

The Climbing Smiths, as they bill themselves, are made up of George, the father; Flint 17, Quade 13, Cody 12, and Tyle 10 years and 31 days. The days of Tyle's age are counted so that his claim of being the youngest boy to ever do this feat won't be challenged.

The Smiths have climbed all of the 53 peaks in Colorado over 14,000 feet, making them part of a small group of 150 who have done so. They started in 1962 when Flint and Quade, then 10 and 6, climbed Mt. Sherman. Cody started in 1964 when he was 7, and Lyle (sic) started in 1966 when he was 6.

Their climb of all the peaks over 14,000 feet made them members of a(n) even smaller group of roughly 25 persons.

After their ascent of Mt. Shasta, which they planned to do in one day, they planned to drive to Rainier, climb it, and then go home.

All of the family are members of the OMC which originally stood for "Own Mountain Club." The original name of the club was conceived when Smith first started climbing while a student at Colorado State University, and didn't have any club name to put down in the registries at the top of mountains. Later they formed a family club with shoulder patches calling it the Outpost Mountain Club.

Smith, a rugged individualist, bought some books on mountaineering when he had nearly finished climbing the peaks in Colorado. Though most experts deplore this, Smith is a person who wanted to do it his own way, and did.

Appendix 6

The Seattle Times - Thursday, September 4, 1969

Family Out of Mountains After Conquering Rainier

By DEE NORTON

George Smith and his four sons completed a climb of Mount Rainier at 4 p. m. yesterday and with it ended a very personal era.

There are 67 mountains in the original 48 states over 14,000 feet. Mount Rainier, 14,410 feet, was the 67th and last one for the Smiths to climb. The Smiths live in Denver.

"It's the end of an era," Smith said. "It was something we looked forward to and I am sad it is over."

His sons are Flint, 17; Quade, 13; Cody, 12, and Tyle, 10.

Rainier caused no unusual problems once they were under way, Smith said.

They were two days late in arriving at the mountain from California, where they had climbed 13 "fourteeners" since August 12.

Yesterday "was a beautiful day and it was a beatiful climb," he said.

"Now we just go home and settle down to be normal people, I guess," Smith said.

Tyle, the youngest son, began climbing "fourteeners" when he was 6. Smith himself began climbing when he was young because his right arm was rendered almost useless by an automobile accident when he was 4.

"I am sure that kind of molded my life," Smith said. He has tried to instill in his sons "the driving force I seem to possess.

"I am devoted to proving that I can do something as well as someone with two good arms," Smith said.

"You sit at the bottom of a mountain and look up at it and you think that it looks too steep to try.

"Then you meet the first problem and you worry about it and not the 10th problem, and as you get to the problems they seem to flatten out."

He believes that each "generation in this country is getting softer. And we are softer with our kids.

"But the problems in this country are not from our kids but their parents," Smith said.

Smith now plans a book. It will include mountain climbing, but more important will be expression of his thoughts on building strong bodies and tough minds.

The Seattle Times, September 4, 1969

246

Appendix 7

- *Items we always took with us: flashlight, matches, extra layer of clothing, some extra food, Swiss army knife, sunglasses, sun cream, first aid kit, water purification, compass, topographical map*
- *Put the heaviest stuff in the bottom of pack near your back to help your balance*
- *Pack water and a rain jacket where you have easy access*
- *Take lemon drops to snack on, suck but don't chew*
- *Before you start, stretch your lungs by taking a deep breath, holding it and then exhaling, repeat several times*
- *Clothing: start walking wearing one layer cold, you will warm up quickly*
- *Don't hike or climb with hands in pockets*
- *Pick up your feet, don't stub toe on rocks or roots, it costs energy*
- *Unsnap your pack's waist belt when crossing a river*
- *Set a pace you can keep all day, don't rush out*
- *Breathe in cadence, vary as it gets steeper, every 4 steps take a breath, every 2 steps take a breath, then every 1 step take a breath*
- *Go as long as you can without stopping, because each stop after the first stop will happen quicker*
- *If we felt the urge to rest, we tried to avoid resting on an uphill stretch. We challenged ourselves to continue hiking until we found a flat spot. Before we got to that flat spot, maybe a "second wind" kicked in and we didn't need to rest. Sometimes we climbed non-stop to the summit*
- *The weather forecast is a useful tool, but you should use experience and common sense in determining whether or not you should continue*
- *If lightning is possible, avoid: 1) ridges, 2) mine shafts, 3) a lone standing tree; plus, move away from metal objects*
- *Eye a destination or landmark to aim for, and another one past that, if possible. When you get there, select the next one. Periodically look back where you came from so the terrain will look familiar on the way down*
- *Don't try to climb up anything that you are unsure you can climb or rappel down*

- *Know how to use a compass and a topographical map*
- *Often what looks steep flattens out as you get closer, you can't tell from here what you'll find up there, get closer*
- *On steep rock keep at least 3 points of contact*
- *Watch out for smaller rocks and sand on flat, large rocks, especially on the way down; they can flip you like you are walking on marbles*
- *The toughest half of a climb is going down. You are heavier, more tired, and possibly distracted because you made it to the top. Pay attention, you are not done until you are down*
- *Night-climbing experience is valuable, it could save your life sometime*
- *If you are planning to climb any of the tougher Colorado peaks, you should know how to belay and rappel, use an ice axe, and know how to tie and use mountaineering knots*

Appendix 8

These thought cards are original with me. That doesn't mean someone else hasn't had a similar thought down through the years:

"If you would teach your children to swim, then for the same reason let them learn the mountains."

"Because of an accident to my right arm early in life, I learned to swim upstream. And, if you can swim upstream, the adversities of life are easier to cope with."

"Everyone has a handicap of some sort, some you can see and some you can't."

"It doesn't take much talent to become a parent, but it takes a whole lot of talent to be a parent."

"I don't know where I am going but I'm a lot further than I was."

"As you travel life's highway, don't be afraid to take the alternate route."

"Nobody ever did anything the first time without doing it for the first time."

"Always leave the gate like you found it."

"Too often a word to the wise is just enough to start an argument."

"Give up? Not yet. You go until you can't go any longer, and then you take one more step."

"Do your best to do your best."

"Keep going. Some of the best memories come from adverse conditions."

"Poor judgement in route finding can be hazardous to your health."

"I can still do a day's work but it might be sometime tomorrow before I am finished."

"You don't learn what is important to learn if you only show up when it's sunny."

"It doesn't cost anything to say 'Thanks'."

"Rather than follow in someone's footsteps, I prefer to make my own."

"Worry on time."

"4 plus 1 = 53."

"Who wants to go climbing?" "Woof!"

"If you say you'll do something, do it. There is nothing more sacred than a man's word."

"I've been in tougher places than this, I just can't remember when."

"I may need to juggle priorities today. I may feel overwhelmed today. I may get discouraged today. But quit? Not today."

"Good judgement comes from experience.... Sometimes experience comes from bad judgement."

"Life is a climb and the route taken determines the rewards."

"Life's journey: Do I have any regrets? Yes, but I have yet to meet anyone I would want to trade places with."

"If you are happy doing what you are doing then you are a success."

Appendix 8

"We are too concerned with quality of life, rather than quality of people."

"We should do a thing because it is a good idea, not because it makes money."

"Don't make a job out of a job."

"Don't hammer with a saw."

"Anything worth doing is worth doing well."

"Today will only happen once. Do some good."

"Leave every day better than you found it, even if no one is watching."

"We are all created equal yet no two of us are alike."

"If you don't have time to do it right in the first place, when will you have time to do it over?"

"Sometimes you suffer a little to learn a lot and sometimes you suffer a lot to learn a little."

"Don't trade easy for best."

"Education costs one or two or three of the following: time, or money, or pain."

"Common sense is the ability to think around the corner."

"The majority of people are passengers in the automobile of life. Only a few are drivers."

"Sometimes the impossible happens."

"It's over there to your right, just out of sight. See it?"

"Be there! It's important that you show up, otherwise we might be one person short."

"If I had it to do over again, I would do it over again."

"The thing that makes us the same is that we are all different."

"Laughter sounds the same no matter what the language."

"The past got you here, but now only the future counts."

"The truly important values in life cost nothing. Teach your kids Love, Honesty, Loyalty, Dependability, and Compassion and they won't give you or society any trouble."

"You can't give your kids too much love but you can give them too much."

"The first step towards failure is to say, 'I can't'."

"Why is it that will power is so hard to muster and common sense is not so common?"

"There are always reasons for mistakes but I don't believe in making excuses."

"Progress: Technology is eroding common sense."

"A close call with death gives one a different slant on life."

"The odds of your not failing are very good if you never try."

"I've told you a thousand times, I don't repeat myself."

"Me? I was born in Colorado at an early age."

"Is there anything you should do or say today in case you're not here tomorrow?"

"On aging: According to statistics I'm old, but I learned a long time ago to not believe everything I read."

"As you get older it's easy to stay busy because it takes longer to do anything."

"If you are anxious for an overdue long-distance phone call, go sit on the john."

"Take my advice and do whatever you want."

"If it's true that one learns from their mistakes, I could become a genius."

"One of these times will be the last time."

"My Lament: Gonna miss this place, gonna miss this place, Lordy, Lordy, gonna miss this place."

References

A Climber's Guide to the High Sierra, Revised Edition, Copyright 1965 by the Sierra Club, Edited by Hervey H. Voge.

Guide to the Colorado Mountains, Copyright 1955 by the Colorado Mountain Club, Edited by Robert M. Ormes.

Mountaineering, the Freedom of the Hills, Second Edition, December 1967, by the Mountaineers.

Starr's Guide to the John Muir Trail and the High Sierra Region, by Walter A. Starr, Jr., June 1964.

About The Author

George Nash Smith was born in Denver in 1928 and is a third-generation Coloradoan. His grandfather, Frank I. Smith, came to Colorado in 1876 to help establish a railroad in Leadville. Due to an unfortunate accident George's right arm and hand were severely injured a month before he was four years old. This traumatic event was life-changing yet became the impetus for his life philosophy, "Not if, but how," which is expressed in this book.

Because he grew up in an emotionally supportive environment, he learned not to use his injury as an excuse. Instead, he learned he could do most everything others could do and developed an attitude of challenging himself. He competed in sports, played a guitar, and climbed mountains.

George joined the Boy Scouts and became an Eagle Scout at age 14. He assumed the role of acting Troop Leader at age 15 during World War II because the troop's Scoutmaster was drafted (see photo 278). He further developed his life philosophy and love for nature through mountain

Photo 278 – George receiving the National Outstanding Eagle Scout Award with his four sons present (from left: Quade, George, Flint, Tyle, Cody) September, 2019

climbing, which began when he and his good friend, Warren Pulis, first climbed Longs Peak while attending college at Colorado A & M in Fort Collins.

George married Marilou Milano in 1951, shortly after she graduated from college. They raised four sons, Flint, Quade, Cody, and Tyle. The boys each became Eagle Scouts, like their Dad, and learned life lessons in the mountains with him. While George and Marilou divorced after the boys were grown, the "Smith kids" are extremely close with each other and their parents to this day.

George became a square dance caller in college and later built a dance hall, called The Outpost, in 1961 where he continues to teach dancing and hold private parties.

Index

Made in the USA
Middletown, DE
13 October 2020

21739354R00155